You're in
Charge Now!

Practical books that inspire

Self-Management and Personal Effectiveness
How to achieve your personal goals in life and at work

Making Meetings Work
How to prepare and run a meeting to get the result you want

Managing Individual Performance
A systematic, seven-step approach to enhancing employee performance and results

Effective Problem-Solving
How to understand the process and practise it successfully

Staying Ahead at Work
How to develop a winning portfolio of work skills and attitudes

howtobooks

Pleae send for a free copy of the latest catalogue to:

How To Books
3 Newtec Place, Magdalen Road
Oxford OX4 1RE, United Kingdom
Tel: (01865) 793806   Fax: (01865) 248780
email: info@howtobooks.co.uk
http://www.howtobooks.co.uk

You're in Charge Now!

The first-time manager's survival kit

JULIE-ANN AMOS

3rd edition

howto books

By the same author

80/20 Management
Be Prepared!
Delegating
Job Hunt on the Net
Managing Your Time
Self-Management and Personal Effectiveness

First published by How To Books Ltd,
3 Newtec Place, Magdalen Road,
Oxford OX4 1RE, United Kingdom.
Tel: (01865) 793806. Fax: (01865) 248780.
email: info@howtobooks.co.uk
http://www.howtobooks.co.uk

British Library Cataloguing in Publication Data.
A catalogue record for this book is available from
the British Library.

Second edition 2000
Third edition 2002

Cartoons by Mike Flanagan
Cover design by Baseline Arts Ltd, Oxford

Produced for How To Books by Deer Park Productions
Typeset by Kestrel Data, Exeter
Printed and bound by Cromwell Press Ltd, Trowbridge, Wiltshire

NOTE: The material contained in this book is set out in good
faith for general guidance and no liability can be accepted
for loss or expense incurred as a result of relying in particular
circumstances on statements made in the book. Laws and
regulations are complex and liable to change, and readers should
check the current position with the relevant authorities before
making personal arrangements.

Contents

List of illustrations

Preface

This book has been written for people who are just starting out as managers. It doesn't include large sections on the various management theories – instead, it concentrates on how to manage. This means things like what to do, what to think about, and what to be aware of.

Each chapter includes some common questions and answers, and has a checklist to remind you of the main points. There are also mini case studies, in which you meet fictional characters, illustrating some points from the chapter – usually how *not* to do it! Lastly, at the end of each chapter you will find some discussion points, to help you apply what you have learned from the text to your own work situation.

I hope you will find the book useful, and that in time, it will help you become a good manager.

Julie-Ann Amos

1

Understanding Management

ARE YOU A MANAGER?

Most dictionaries define management as 'being in charge of', 'controlling', or 'administering'. Basically, you are a manager if you have a measure of control over any of the following:

- time
- workloads
- decisions
- technology
- equipment
- money
- standards
- meetings
- other people.

Outside of work everyone is a manager, because everyone manages their own life: money, time and decisions. But in work, we often don't think of ourselves as a manager until we have some form of control and/or authority over other people.

MANAGING OR SUPERVISING?

Supervising
The word supervisor comes from the Latin words

'super' = over

and

'visor' = to see.

Thus, 'supervisor' = overseer. A supervisor's job is to oversee one or more of the list of things above: to inspect and monitor them.

Managing

A manager has a wider picture. Not only do they inspect and monitor things now, but it is also usually their job to make predictions, to plan ahead, and to decide how things will change and develop. A manager also generally reviews the past when planning and forecasting the future. Thus, the difference between the two is perhaps their viewpoints: the supervisor is often mainly concerned with the present, and the manager with future, present and past.

WHAT DO MANAGERS DO?

There are many functions which a manager carries out. A sample of these are:

- control
- taking responsibility
- setting objectives and/or goals
- organisation
- delegation
- accepting authority
- decision-making
- support
- communications
- training

- monitoring/evaluating
- leadership
- motivation
- planning.

The list is not exhaustive: how many more can you think of?

BALANCING MANAGEMENT

Imagine you are shipwrecked. There are a dozen of you in a liferaft, looking for land. *You* are elected to stand at the front of the boat, keeping a good lookout for land. After a long hard day of your colleagues rowing, you can see land on the horizon, and you encourage them to row towards it as hard as they can. However, when you get closer, you realise three things:

- There are rocks and reefs between you and the land.
- A strong tide is threatening to sweep you off course, and straight past the land.
- Your shipmates are dangerously tired now, and may not have the strength to reach the land unless you take an oar yourself, and help them row. What is more, they are beginning to grumble nastily about you 'not pulling your weight', and leaving them to do all the work.

So, what do you do? For here you have it in a nutshell: the balancing act that is management. Do you pitch in and help the others, and risk losing the overview (which only you fully understand)? Or, do you stay in control and risk alienating the workforce? One thing is certain; the decision isn't straightforward or easy.

WEIGHING UP THE OPTIONS

Most managerial functions operate in pairs, and a manager needs to balance the two extremes, leaning towards one or the other as and when appropriate. On the following pages you will see some of the main balances of management illustrated in Figures 1 to 7. These are:

- Control v. motivation

- Procedures v. flexibility

- Progress v. stability

- Delegation v. personal control

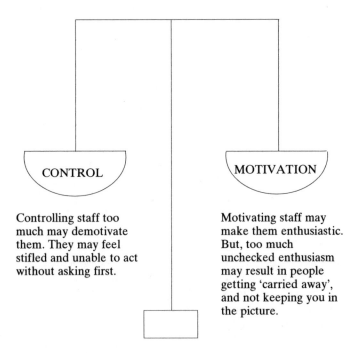

Controlling staff too much may demotivate them. They may feel stifled and unable to act without asking first.

Motivating staff may make them enthusiastic. But, too much unchecked enthusiasm may result in people getting 'carried away', and not keeping you in the picture.

Fig. 1. Control v. motivation.

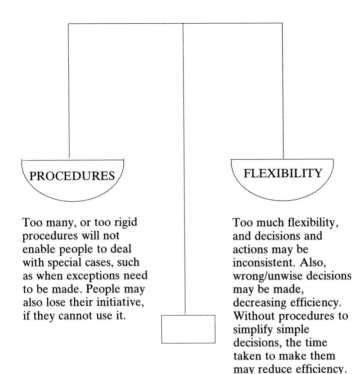

PROCEDURES

Too many, or too rigid procedures will not enable people to deal with special cases, such as when exceptions need to be made. People may also lose their initiative, if they cannot use it.

FLEXIBILITY

Too much flexibility, and decisions and actions may be inconsistent. Also, wrong/unwise decisions may be made, decreasing efficiency. Without procedures to simplify simple decisions, the time taken to make them may reduce efficiency.

Fig. 2. Procedures v. flexibility.

- Responsibility v. authority
- Security v. risk-taking
- Logic v. inspiration.

Hard, isn't it? We want, as managers, to do all these things, but to balance them so we don't focus too much on any one thing and suffer as a result of ignoring its partner.

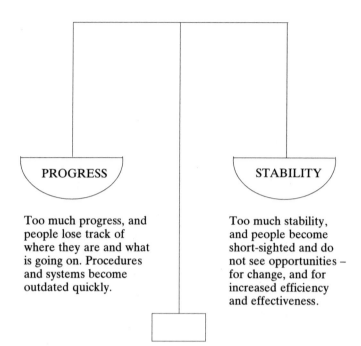

Fig. 3. Progress v. stability.

QUESTIONS AND ANSWERS

So is balancing management about 'sitting on the fence'?
Not at all. No one is suggesting that you 'sit on the fence'
at all times and keep balanced exactly in the middle.
Nobody has an equal balance of everything: we all have
natural tendencies – for example, to favour progress and
change, or to prefer stability and the status quo. What
is important is realising that your usual way of doing
things is not the only way, neither will it always be
appropriate.

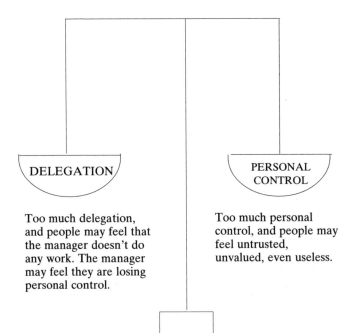

Fig. 4. Delegation v. personal control.

So how does this help me be a better manager?
By learning about good management. Read this book and
others – a useful list of further reading can be found at the
back of this book. Look at yourself and where you work.
See how things could be improved, and also where things
are working well. Use what you read to help you make
changes to your approach and the way you do things,
where you can.

*So do I need to learn about management theories to manage
well?*
Not necessarily. They can help you understand what is
happening at work, and why, and how things might be

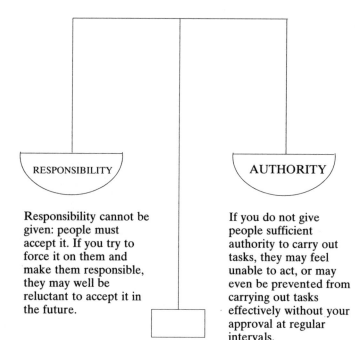

Fig. 5. Responsibility v. authority.

improved. But you need to remember that a theory is just that – a *theory*. A theory is an idea, not a fact, and therefore it may not work for you, in your place of work. For this reason, wherever possible, this book concentrates on practical ways of doing things, rather than theories.

RECOGNISING MANAGEMENT STYLES

Your style of managing will depend on four main influences:

20

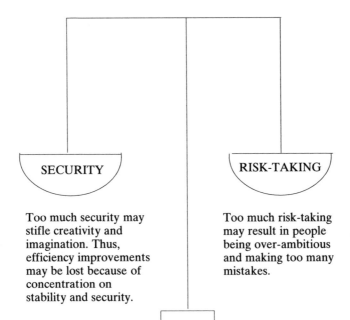

SECURITY

Too much security may
stifle creativity and
imagination. Thus,
efficiency improvements
may be lost because of
concentration on
stability and security.

RISK-TAKING

Too much risk-taking
may result in people
being over-ambitious
and making too many
mistakes.

Fig. 6. Security v. risk-taking.

1. yourself

2. other people working with or around you

3. the situation

4. constraints imposed by your organisation and/or
workplace.

You may have one style which you tend naturally to adopt,
or your style may vary depending on how the mixture of
the four ingredients varies. However, there seem to be six
main styles of management.

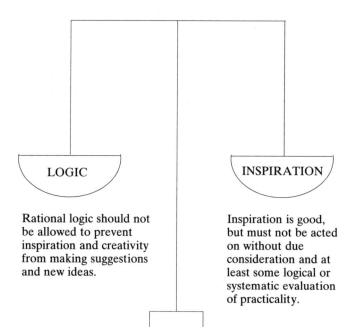

Fig. 7. Logic v. inspiration.

CHOOSING A MANAGEMENT STYLE

Being authoritarian

The *authoritarian* manager dictates, and tells people what to do.

Good points
- People submit to the manager's leadership.

- The manager is always in control.

Bad points
- People are dependent on the manager.

- People are insecure, unproductive, and have little or no initiative without the manager.

Being persuading

A manager with a *persuading* style is like a parent in the way they treat people. They make the decisions, and then try to persuade people that this is the best course of action.

Good points
- People generally feel less dominated than with an authoritarian manager.

- Some people may like this level of control and care.

Bad points
- Some people may resent the manager, as they are not treated as adults.

- The manager may feel hurt if people fail, as if they have been 'let down'.

Being consulting

With a *consulting* manager, people are welcome to contribute ideas, suggestions etc, and the manager discusses these and then makes the decision.

Good points
- People feel involved.

- People feel part of a team, and feel valued.

Bad points
- People may resent decisions if their own suggestions were unsuccessful.

- People may try to challenge the manager's decision.

Being democratic

With a *democratic* manager, the manager and others all take part in work. Decisions are made by the whole group, and the manager agrees to abide by these, as long as they are within any boundaries or constraints imposed by the workplace and/or organisation.

Good points
- Individuals feel enthusiastic, and tend to take responsibility readily.

- Communication and teamwork are good.

Bad points
- The manager needs to have complete confidence in people.

- The manager can lose control.

Being a delegator

The *delegating* manager sets limits, and gives problems, work etc to others, who refer back on difficulties, but otherwise take on the entire task as their own.

Good points
- Work is efficient.

- Individuals are given experience of a wide variety of work.

Bad points
- Individuals may feel overburdened with responsibility.

- The manager may not be available to help when problems arise.

Being an abdicator

The manager *abdicates* – opts out – by becoming so involved in their own work that others are left to their own devices. Often, managers do this because they mistakenly think they are delegating.

Good points
- The manager is free to get on with their own work.

24

Bad points
- People blame the manager, even when it is their own fault.

- Work is poor, morale is low, and people feel frustrated and resentful.

MANAGEMENT TIPS

- Be aware that management is a balancing act.

- Try to avoid too narrow a focus on any one thing.

- Aim for an appropriate style, without being too authoritarian, or abdicating.

- Always try to remember: how would you feel if your boss behaved exactly like you?

CASE STUDIES – AN INTRODUCTION

Let us introduce you to three managers whom you will be looking at in the following chapters. Each is different, and has gained their present position via a different route. We will observe how they handle a variety of situations.

Bev Hall, Shift Manager
Bev Hall is in her late forties, and has worked at the same nursing home on the south coast for twelve years. Before that, she worked in other similar homes for the elderly. She has never received any management or supervisory training, but because of her age and experience, has always been looked to for advice by other staff. A year ago, a new Matron made changes to the organisation of the home, and Bev was made Shift Manager. She now has management responsibility for twelve Care Assistants, two Domestics, plus a Cook. She feels that these resent her new position, and does not like having an office to work in, rather than being 'out and about'.

Nikki Coates, Office Manager
Nikki Coates is twenty-two, and recently gained an internal promotion to the busy head office of a large retail company. She is friendly, and seems to 'get on' well with her staff of five, but sometimes worries as to whether she is managing the office as well as it could be managed. Her predecessor had a management qualification, and although Nikki has a qualification in Administration, she feels it did not prepare her for dealing with the day-to-day difficulties of managing a hectic office.

Mike Summers, Corporate Accounting Manager
Mike Summers is a graduate. Having gained his university degree in Accountancy, he gained his first job as manager of a four-strong Corporate Accounts section of a local authority. Three of his staff are studying for their accountancy qualifications by day release or correspondence course, and he is aware that although he is better qualified, they know far more about the section and how it works than he does. He feels that he needs to take control of the team, and stamp his authority on it, if he is to be respected and taken seriously.

ACTION POINTS

1. Think of a good manager you have known. Why were they good?

2. Think of a bad manager you have known. Have you ever done any of the things you didn't like about *their* management?

3. Which management style fits you most of the time? Could this be improved on?

2

Managing Workloads

MANAGING TIME

Time cannot be managed. It can't be increased or
decreased, delegated, reallocated, saved or lost.
Everybody, no matter who they are, has the same amount
of it available to them every day. What is more, it is one of
the few things in this world that you can waste, misuse,
throw away or lose without it bearing a grudge – tomorrow
you will still get the same amount of it, no matter how
badly you spend it today.

What you can't do, however, is turn back the clock and
get back what you lost or wasted yesterday.

BEING EFFECTIVE AND EFFICIENT

Management is about both effectiveness and efficiency.
Good time management means we aim to be both.
However, it is important to realise that they are not the
same.

EFFECTIVE = Doing the right things

EFFICIENT = Doing something in the right way

You can be both, neither, or just one, as the table in Fig. 8
shows. First, we are going to look at how to be **effective:**
how to make sure we do the right things, and don't spend
our time doing the wrong ones. That may sound rather
basic, but very rarely do we actually look at *what* we do –
our effectiveness. Many people spend far more time
looking at efficiency – *how* we do things, and ways of doing

	EFFECTIVE	NOT EFFECTIVE
EFFICIENT	Doing the right things in the right way or well	Doing the wrong things well
NOT EFFICIENT	Doing the right things in the wrong way, or badly	Doing the wrong things badly

Fig. 8. Efficiency or effectiveness?

things in the best way. The rest of the book will help you there, but first, let's take a look at effectiveness.

RECORDING YOUR TIME

You cannot improve how you spend your time unless you know what you spend it on. So, you need to measure what you are spending your time doing at present. Keep a time log for at least ten working days, preferably a month. In this, you will list everything you do and for how long. Include all those cups of coffee and telephone calls both made and received – everything you do.

At the end of the recording period, do some sums on where your time went. Analyse how much time was spent on each activity. When you have the totals, you may well be surprised at just how much of your time certain things take.

Ask yourself some general questions, and try to be objective and honest about the results:

1. What time of day did I get the most achieved? What time of day did I get the least achieved?

2. How much time was spent on inefficiency – waiting, looking for things, being interrupted etc?

3. How much time did I spend on tasks that were unnecessary?

4. How much time did I spend on tasks I could or should have got somebody else to do?

5. Did I achieve all the things I needed to? If not, why not?

ASSESSING EFFECTIVENESS

Now, let's take a closer look at that list. If you were to go through your results and make one long list of every single task you did, e.g. making phone calls, answering mail, attending a meeting, writing a report, reading etc, it would tell you what your workload was for the period of the time recorded.

Make out a list for your current workload. Write down *everything* you have to do, including routine things, and things already started. We are going to work on your workload, and see how effective you are.

Step 1 – delegating

'D' stands for delegate. Mark a big 'D' by any activities which shouldn't be done by you. Over a period of time, work towards delegating these to a more appropriate person wherever possible. You may find it easier delegating things you don't like doing, but dislike delegating things you enjoy. Well, there's nothing wrong with keeping a few tasks that are enjoyable, but not strictly speaking part of your job. Just resist the temptation to keep too many.

Step 2 – pruning

Now look for any tasks which really shouldn't be done at all – by anyone. Mark them with an 'X'. Again, over a period of time, you should try to eliminate these wherever possible. There may always be a small number of tasks that your boss or other senior people require you to do that are, in your opinion, unnecessary. You may be stuck with these, but there is no harm in politely pointing out your views.

Step 3 – prioritising

Everything that is left unmarked should be done by you, if you have done your list correctly. Now prioritise these. Put an 'A' by tasks that are high priority – essential to your job and objectives, or to the objectives of your organisation. Put a 'B' by medium priority tasks. These are less important than 'A' tasks, and are not essential, although they may be important.

Step 4 – identifying lower priorities

Put a 'C' by low priority tasks. These are tasks that are supposed to be done, but would not cause major problems if they weren't. Check carefully to see whether any could be delegated, and change them to a 'D', delegating them if it is possible to.

Step 5 – separating the lists

You now have a list of your own tasks. Once you have eliminated the 'X' tasks and the 'D' tasks, these are the only things you should be spending your time on. Separate these remaining tasks into three separate lists – so you have an 'A' list, a 'B' list and a 'C' list. Some managers just operate one list, marking it 'A', 'B' or 'C' as appropriate, but to start with you will probably find it easier to operate three separate lists.

Step 6 – choosing an order

So, your highest priority is to get the 'A' tasks done. Or is it? Take a few minutes to go through all three lists, and remember, you have all these tasks to do yourself. For each task, mark items with a 'U' if they are urgent, and an 'I' if they are important. Some tasks will be neither, some will be both: it's rather like effectiveness and efficiency – they are not the same.

CASE STUDY

Bev learns that effectiveness is not the same as efficiency

Matron asks Bev to make out duty lists. These are lists of tasks that need to be done by the care assistants. Each list is to be copied and given out at the beginning of the shift, and people will sign it to say they have completed tasks. Bev does this, and the lists are signed each day. After a week, Matron carries out an inspection. 'Bev, the home is disgraceful!' she says. 'Standards have never been so bad – whatever is going wrong? You'll have to make sure things improve. I'll inspect again in two days time, and things had better be up to scratch.'

Bev was horrified – she had standard lists of tasks to be done each day, which people signed to say all tasks were completed. However, focusing on tasks to be done on a day-to-day basis meant that tasks weren't being prioritised. She could have concentrated more on *how* things were being done and less on *whether* they were being done at all. Ticks in boxes don't mean things are done properly, or that the most important things are given sufficient time and attention.

ASSESSING IMPORTANCE AND URGENCY

Understanding importance

Important tasks are – guess what? – *important*. That means you need to spend enough time on them to make sure you get them right.

	URGENT	NOT URGENT
IMPORTANT	'UI' – Important *and* Urgent – do immediately, taking sufficient time to get the task done well	'I' – Important, but can wait
NOT IMPORTANT	'U' – do quickly, but spend as little time as possible on these	Leave until last

Fig. 9. Importance or urgency?

Understanding urgency

Urgent tasks are not necessarily important, so get them out of the way quickly: they usually don't have to be perfect, they just have to be done – *urgently*. Fig. 9 shows the difference between important and urgent tasks.

Deciding on an order

You can see that you obviously need to do tasks marked 'UI' and 'U' first. Are they all on the 'A' list? Probably not. The fact is that just because a task is low priority, it doesn't mean it isn't urgent. So, get it out of the way quickly.

It is largely a matter of personal taste, but a good rule for deciding what order to do tasks in would probably be as follows:

- U tasks – A list, then B, then C
- UI tasks – A list, then B, then C

- I tasks – A list, then B, then C
- Unmarked tasks remaining.

Doesn't it look simple when you see it like that?

Planning big tasks

Sometimes, tasks are too large to be done at one sitting. So, watch out for this, and when you find such tasks, break them into smaller steps and add these to the lists, coding them appropriately and crossing off the big overall task.

QUESTIONS AND ANSWERS

But this all takes time. Surely if I did all this before starting work I wouldn't have much time left for anything else?
Not at all. You are *investing* time at the beginning, to *save* time later. Your A/B/C lists (let's call them your TO DO lists) only have to be set up once, then you add to them every day, crossing things off as you complete them. In return for the time invested at the beginning, you will spend less time deciding what to do next, jumping from task to task, dealing with interruptions, or even worrying about how to get it all done. But you must update your lists *every day*: what was not urgent yesterday may have become urgent today.

Won't my lists just keep getting longer and longer?
Yes and no. They will get longer as new tasks are added: every time the telephone rings and a new task comes your way, or the morning post brings more work, you simply add it to your lists. But they get shorter as you complete tasks and cross them off, or delegate them. And just think of all the peace of mind you would get from knowing you can't forget to do something or miss a deadline, because it is all on your list to make sure you remember.

So how do I add in all the new tasks that come my way?
Just add them to the appropriate TO DO list, either A, B
or C, and mark them urgent and/or important, then they
can be dealt with as appropriate. If possible, carry on and
finish the task you are doing before starting any new one,
unless it really cannot wait. Also, always remember that a
lot of quick, low priority, urgent tasks, such as telephone
calls or arranging meetings or appointments, could perhaps
be delegated in a block to someone with more time and/or
fewer tasks.

SCHEDULING AND DIARISING

So far, we have talked about prioritising and planning, and
what order to do tasks in. This was effectiveness – doing
the right things in the right order. Scheduling and diarising
is one thing that will help you be more **efficient** – doing
things well. So how do you decide exactly *when* to do tasks?

Individual tastes vary as to what type of diary is best,
and there are many sorts available. There are also many
personal organisers which combine diaries with TO DO
lists. Whichever you use, the following list of points will be
applicable, and will help you use your diary to best
advantage.

Practical tips

Scheduling time
Plan and schedule your time on a weekly and daily basis –
this means you need to set aside a small amount of time to
do this every day, and every week.

Keep some time back
Never schedule all your time – always keep some reserved
for urgent tasks that arise.

Update daily
Take a small amount of time *every day* in the morning to

update your TO DO lists and preview that day's tasks.
Carry forward tasks not completed yesterday, and if you
end up with too long a list of tasks for today, delegate
some, or move them on in your schedule.

Transfer from TO DO lists to diary
Schedule tasks from your TO DO lists into your diary. This
may seem like a waste of time, but it is vital. If you and
others see blank space in your diary, you will think you
have spare time to take on more tasks. You don't –
remember all the things on your lists and more coming
your way all the time? So, at the start of every day, use
some time to decide which items to do when, and book
them into the diary.

This really is important – until now we have decided
what to do, but now you are making sure you keep the
time free to do things *when* they need doing. So remember
to book in your scheduling and updating time every
morning. Think of it as a meeting between three parties –
yourself, your TO DO lists and your diary. If you had an
appointment with your boss, you would probably put it in
your diary so you would remember it. Well, you have an
appointment with a task once it is in your diary – it is a
major key to getting things done on time.

Remember timing
Schedule important tasks when you will be at your best.
This will be a different time for everyone – some people
work better early in the day, others later.

Respect other people's time
Don't be late or break appointments at the last minute
unless it is absolutely unavoidable. It disrupts other
people's schedules, and they may do the same to you.

Travelling and waiting
Use travelling and waiting time productively – always have
something with you that you can do in a spare five
minutes, so time isn't wasted.

Routine calls and correspondence
Allow time for making telephone calls and dealing with
routine correspondence. Book this time like an
appointment – that way you know you will have time to do
them.

Setting deadlines
If a task has no deadline, set your own, on the basis of its
priority. Then enter it in your diary in the usual way.

CASE STUDY

Nikki learns about priorities – and responsibilities
Nikki keeps a diary, in which she schedules meetings,
deadlines and tasks. She also keeps a record of what her
staff are doing. One Monday she take an important call
from a senior manager, asking for some figures for a
management report on Friday. She checks the diary and
allocates the work. 'It's not urgent, Bill, but I do need it by
the end of the week.' On Tuesday, Bill has more urgent
tasks. On Wednesday, the computer system breaks down,
and work has to be done manually. On Thursday, Nikki
speaks to everyone. 'We've got a day's computer input to
catch up on, as well as keeping up with today's work. I
want you to leave everything that's not urgent, so we can
catch up.' Bill of course leaves the figures – after all,
they're not urgent. On Friday morning, when the
manager calls, the figures aren't done and Nikki feels
stupid.

She should have told Bill why they were needed, so he
could have prioritised them correctly. She should also have
checked what work really was urgent when the situation
changed and everything was disrupted, and that particular
piece of work would never have been left.

AVOIDING STRESS

Stress is a large topic. In the following paragraphs, you will find a few simple pointers about managing workloads that will help you avoid stress.

Practical tips

Meeting deadlines
Meet deadlines wherever possible. Stress is not caused by all the things we do – it is caused by all the work we *don't* do, preying on our minds and building up pressure.

Setting goals
Set realistic goals – accept that you cannot do everything, especially not all at once.

Sleeping
Find out what your minimum sleep requirement is. Make sure you get it. Working too late often means you get insufficient sleep, as you go home after work and try to fit your home life into a shorter space of time. This either makes you pressured at home, which may stop you sleeping, or you may end up staying up longer. Insufficient sleep just means you work slower and less well the next day: it would be more efficient to sleep more and work better.

Taking 'time out'
Always take a little 'time out' to think, listen, relax, take a walk etc – whatever works for you – to unwind from the pressures of the day. Taking a coffee break may do this, but too much caffeine from tea and/or coffee can just 'wind you up' again.

Being realistic
Recognise your limitations, and try not to take on things you either can't do, or don't have sufficient time to do. Set or agree to realistic goals and deadlines only.

Staying organised
Keep your office or workspace well organised. This doesn't mean tidy, it means *organised* – so both you and others can find things without wasting time and getting into a panic.

Taking time off
Plan holidays and time off well in advance, and stick to them.

UNDERSTANDING DELEGATION

Delegation is giving someone (usually a subordinate) the authority to carry out a task. They are *accountable* for the task, and can make decisions relating to it (within any limits that are set), but the manager keeps the overall responsibility.

Remember effectiveness and efficiency? Well, the most effective managers spend their time doing only the tasks that only they can do. They delegate the rest.

Advantages
- The manager has more time.

- The manager is free for planning, creative work, and for *managing* – which is, after all, what they are paid for.

- Staff are developed – they develop new skills, and use their existing skills fully.

- Staff are involved, and therefore happier and more satisfied in their work.

- Morale is good.

- Decisions are often better, as they are made by the people 'closest to the action'.

- Time is saved. Delays while people wait for your decision are eliminated – they decide for themselves.

- You are protected in the event of absence (holidays,

sickness etc) as your work can go on, simply being
delegated in your absence.

Disadvantages

- Some managers fear losing control. Avoid this by
  making the other person's limits of authority clear, and
  checking on them occasionally.

- Some managers fear the task will be done less well:
  'they wouldn't do it as well as me'. Probably not at first,
  but in time and with help, it will be done just as well as
  you could, but without you doing any work. Just think
  of all the time you could save!

- Some staff may constantly refer back, to check things
  are proceeding satisfactorily. Avoid this by briefing
  them properly, and try to encourage 'management by
  exception'. This is where you are not informed if things
  are going normally, only if things are exceptionally
  good or bad.

- People may feel 'put upon'. Avoid this by spreading out
  your delegation. Even if one person is better than the
  others, do not overload them: delegate to the others, so
  they have a chance to become good too.

- Some managers are afraid the other person will do a
  better job than them. Well, good! Let them produce
  good work, and you do the same with the work *you*
  are good at. This is efficiency – doing things in the best
  way.

DELEGATING PROPERLY

Familiarisation

Get to know people – not just what they can do already,
but what they would like to learn to do. Try to match
delegated tasks to individuals if possible.

Limitations
Know the limits. Ask yourself:

- What do you want?
- To what standard?
- How will you judge or measure the result?
- What are the constraints – time?
  - money?
  - resources?
  - staff?
- How much authority do you give the other person?
- What do you want them to refer back to you on, and when?

Briefing
Brief the other person properly. Tell them the answers to the above list, so they know exactly what's going on.

Authorising
Brief others that you are delegating this task, so they know what authority you have given to the person it is delegated to.

Training
Train people if necessary. This does not have to be a training course – show them, explain, or get them to talk to someone else who has done it before.

Availability
Be available. Don't cut yourself off so people can't ask for help if they need it.

Checking
Check on progress or results as planned. Do not over-check: let people 'get on with it', but check on them at agreed intervals.

CASE STUDY

Mike does too much checking

Mike likes to delegate. He accepts work coming in, and reallocates it to one of his team, keeping himself free to check and monitor progress. He sets progress deadlines, and regularly asks how things are going. When he is away at a meeting, some work is sent out with several errors. Without him there to check, his team's work can't be guaranteed to come up to standard. And yet, they're all good people.

Mike should delegate properly, and offer his people some control and responsibility over their tasks. Checking their work all the time means that they get demotivated, and have no incentive to produce high quality work. Then when he isn't there to check, errors which he would have picked up are missed. By not truly delegating, he never really lets his staff control their tasks.

MANAGEMENT TIPS

- Carry out a time-recording exercise periodically, to check you are not developing bad habits.

- Constantly check and update your TO DO list: tasks that are not urgent will become more and more urgent the longer you leave them.

- Take time to prioritise, so you do things in the right order.

- Be sensible – don't subject yourself to unnecessary stress.

- Delegate as much as possible, but taking time to train and brief people properly.

- Try to discourage staff 'delegating upwards' *their* tasks or decisions to you – unless it really is necessary.

- Beware of wasting other people's time, for example by being late. It will only encourage them to do it to you.

- Say 'no' to tasks that shouldn't be yours, and direct them to the appropriate person.

ACTION POINTS

1. Where did each of the three managers in the case studies go wrong?

2. What things do you do that would be better delegated, or handled differently?

3. Who delegates work to you? Is it all suitable, or would someone else be better placed to do it?

3

Managing Problems and Making Decisions

LOOKING AT PROBLEMS AND DECISIONS

In this chapter, we will look at decision-making and problem-solving. Of course, not all decisions you make are in answer to a problem – many will be simply a matter of trying to choose the best from a number of alternatives. However, because of the links between decision-making and problem-solving, we will look at them together.

Whenever you have a problem to be solved or an issue to be decided upon, there is a logical sequence you can follow to ensure the right decision is made and implemented.

1. Define the problem or issue.
2. Gather information.
3. Create options.
4. Evaluate options.
5. Make the decision(s).
6. Implement the decision(s).
7. Follow up and evaluate.

DEFINING PROBLEMS OR ISSUES

Whatever the problem or issue is, take some time to think about it. Problems do not solve themselves, nor do decisions make themselves, so do not fall into the trap of leaving things alone and hoping they will sort themselves out. This is *not* 'thinking about it', it is *procrastination* – putting things off – the sign of an ineffectual manager. Simply think the matter through thoroughly.

43

Define problems or issues carefully, and preferably in writing. The problem you are initially faced with, or the issue that needs a decision, may not actually be at the heart of the matter. Let me explain.

Problems v. solutions

Let's say your boss asks you to improve the accuracy of some work – there are too many errors. What is the problem? Most people in this situation would say that the problem or issue is how to improve accuracy. Wrong! Improving accuracy is the *solution* – the desired outcome. So what is the problem? You don't know!

Although this may seem a little strange at first, very often you will find that the problem you are faced with is actually a solution. It is then up to you to define the problem. Try drawing a diagram, or writing out a list of possible problems, then find out which is the real one, or the most likely. For example:

Problem   *Solution*
Lack of time   Improved accuracy
Poor standards
Bored, inattentive staff
Work too difficult
Staff poorly trained or untrained
Unclear objectives
Poor materials
Faulty equipment
etc etc

From this, you can quickly decide which problem or problems are the cause. Then, specifically define the problem and desired outcome in writing. For example:

Problem – Lack of time and demotivated staff.
Desired outcome – Improved accuracy.

Fig. 10. Most problems have a social and technical aspect.

Social v. technical

It is also helpful to remember that most problems or issues have two aspects: social and technical. Think of crabs and lobsters. Crabs and lobsters are both caught in fishing pots, even though their strong claws make them perfectly capable of climbing out. But they don't, so they stay caught! Why? What exactly is the problem? (See Fig. 10.)

Crabs

Crabs try to climb out, scrambling and climbing on and over each other in the process. Sometimes one will succeed, but their problem is that as one crab nears escape, the others will grab it and pull it back down in their own bid for freedom. They just don't co-operate. If they left each other alone, they could climb out one at a time. Their problem is **social**.

Lobsters

Lobsters don't even seriously try. They never look up, so they keep trying to find a way out through the side of the pot, and almost never climb up to freedom. Their problem is **technical**.

Consider the previous example. The social part of the problem is that staff are demotivated. The technical part is that they haven't sufficient time to do the job properly. No one is saying that the two things aren't related – one reason why the staff are demotivated may well be because they are rushed, and they know they are producing poor work, but this doesn't have to be the case. Not every single issue or problem you look at will have both social and technical aspects, but a large percentage of them will, so it is worth remembering.

Once you have defined exactly what the problem is, write it down. This will prevent you becoming sidetracked.

GATHERING INFORMATION

You need to find out about things. Perhaps you still can't be sure exactly what the real problem is, until you have done some investigation. Start looking for information about the situation, to help you prepare to create options and make a decision.

Remember the quality of information
When gathering information, always make written notes of what you learn, so it cannot be confused or forgotten. Keep a record of everything, and it is often helpful to remember that the *quality* of information is as important as the *quantity*.

Facts
Facts are things that are known to be true. They are provable and reliable.

Deductions
Deductions (or conclusions) are thoughts based on facts. They are logically derived from and supported by facts, but

unlike facts cannot be directly proved, only concluded (if they can be proven, they are a fact, not a deduction). As information, therefore, they do not have the same worth as facts: if you had two pieces of information, one fact and one deduction, the fact should have more importance in your thinking.

Opinions
Opinions are thoughts, based on information which may include facts, but which is not completely factual. An opinion is a belief or judgement, and cannot be proved. As information, opinions are the least important.

Remember the source of information
Also bear in mind the *source* of a piece of information. Something from an original source – 'from the horse's mouth' – is more reliable than information which has been passed on via someone else, especially if passed by word of mouth.

Points to remember
Keep in mind the following points when you gather information:

- Do I need more information?
- Does this information lead me to more?
- Have I missed anything?
- Is there a pattern evolving?
- Is the situation social, technical, or both?

You don't need to do lengthy research in books and documents – talking to people is an excellent way of gathering information, and will make people feel they are involved in the decision-making process. This is important, because people are more likely to be helpful and supportive of your decision if they feel they had some part in it.

Time wasting

Don't spend so much time gathering information that you skimp on time to evaluate options and make the decision. Some managers become absorbed in the information, using this as a subconscious means of putting off making a difficult decision – procrastination again.

CASE STUDY

Mike fails to check the quality of information

Mike has a problem tracking down the reason why some figures are not as expected, and asks everyone what they think. Rachel says, 'I don't know. Usually things like that are down to the manager in that department making a mistake.' Tom says, 'Last time it was computer error.' Jo says she will have a look and see what she can come up with, and Sam says, 'Hold on a minute, I think I can remember someone telephoning about this – I think the budget was amended.' Mike writes a stern memo to the budget manager, asking him to come up with an explanation. The next thing he knows, the man is on the telephone in a temper. Apparently, the computer has entered some items in the wrong categories, and he's been unable to undo the error.

Mike should have remembered to check the quality of his information, to avoid embarrassment. Just because Sam's idea sounded factual, he jumped at it, and didn't really investigate any of the alternatives. Had he researched, he would have found that the computer *was* making an error in this case.

CREATING OPTIONS

The purpose of creating options is to give you a number of possible options, alternatives or solutions, from which you can make your decision. You do not have to do this alone – you can get several people or a group to look at an issue and generate options. This has the advantage of 'several heads being better than one', and minimises the likelihood of you overlooking something.

The main methods of creating options are logical thinking and creative thinking.

Using logical thinking

Logical thinking is also known as convergent thinking, vertical thinking, analytical thinking or deductive reasoning. It is a process of logical deduction. You take known facts or other information, and draw deductions from them to arrive at a solution.

Advantages

- The solution is beyond doubt the right one.

- Good for solving technical problems.

Disadvantages

- There may be insufficient information to draw conclusions and deductions from.

- There may not be only one right answer.

- The 'right answer' arrived at may not be the *best* answer.

Using creative thinking

Creative thinking uses the imagination to make opinions and deductions from information that may be factual, but may not. It is also known as divergent thinking, lateral thinking or bisociative thinking.

Advantages

- Options can be generated without any facts.

- More options can be generated than by logical thinking.

- More factors can be taken into account.

Disadvantages
- People can find it hard to think creatively, especially when they are used to working analytically.

- Because the options are not always based on facts, they may turn out to be wrong when more facts are known.

- Options and decisions may not be taken seriously by others, without the backup of facts and logic.

Brainstorming

There are several creative thinking techniques, but the most popular is brainstorming – a process of imaginative suggestion. A group of people are encouraged to come up with ideas or suggestions, regardless of how silly or impractical they can be. Ideas are not judged, criticised or evaluated in any way, so people feel free to use their imaginations and be creative. A relaxed, light-hearted atmosphere will encourage people to 'bounce ideas around'.

Record *every* option the group comes up with – even if it is impossibly impractical. This is important, because even ideas that are no good themselves may still be of value, as they may make other ideas occur to people, and these resulting ideas may themselves be useful.

Once a large number of ideas has been generated, they can be evaluated and narrowed down to good suggestions.

Advantages
- Produces a large quantity of options.

- Motivates people.

- Can build working relationships between the people in the group.

Disadvantages
- Some people find it difficult to suspend criticism and judgement.

- The leader of the session must be careful to keep things 'on track'.

- A session can degenerate into a frivolous atmosphere, where people don't take things seriously.

Comparing logical and creative thinking

Logical, analytical thinking often doesn't give imagination a chance. People are often trained in logical thinking at school and other stages in their learning, but rarely in creative thinking. Creative thinking can therefore be difficult for many people.

What are the barriers to creative thinking?

- People think they can't be creative – they have 'mental blocks'.

- People believe there is one right answer.

- People want to conform, so they give options they think will be acceptable or well-received.

- People are lazy – they accept the obvious, and don't look for other options.

- People want to get the issue out of the way, so they evaluate too quickly.

- People are afraid of being 'wrong' and looking foolish.

Encouraging creative thinking

There are four main ways to encourage creative thinking:

1. *Suspend judgement* – give and allow no criticism.

2. *'Freewheel'* – the wilder the ideas the better. Let people come up with anything they want.

3. *Quality not quantity* – the more ideas the better.

4. *Combining* – an idea isn't just left as it is. Combine ideas and build on ideas to make others.

Groups v. individuals

Whether to use a group of people or your own judgement to make decisions is a choice you may face. Each has its own advantages and disadvantages.

Individual problem-solving
- An expert usually knows best.

- It tends to be quicker.

- Individuals tend to have their ideas 'dry up' quicker than groups.

- Narrow thinking can limit the options generated.

- Stress can be high – it is lonely 'carrying the can' for a decision.

Group problem-solving
- Better than average solutions are usually achieved.

- Discussions can get out of hand.

- More ideas can be generated.

- People may be upset if their idea is rejected.

- Solutions can take longer to produce.

- Solutions tend to be more accurate.

CASE STUDY

Nikki needs to be more creative

Nikki is asked to come up with a range of options for producing a new corporate booklet. She gives the job to Peter, who has worked on similar projects before, and he decides on a format. Nikki goes to her Senior Management Team meeting and does a short presentation on the format, but no one likes it. She is sent away to come up with more ideas – several this time.

Peter may have had experience, but using just one

person's ideas isn't likely to lead to very creative ideas. Involving more people would have generated more ideas, and maybe Peter's idea could have been improved on. Had Nikki come up with a range of options as she was originally asked, and not just one, Peter's same idea might have been the best one, and might even have been accepted.

QUESTIONS AND ANSWERS

So does it matter which type of thinking I use?
Yes. If there is only one correct answer, or where facts are involved, logical (analytical) thinking is best. But where imagination is required, or to generate options from which you can choose the *best* answer, creative thinking is best.

Why is it sometimes so hard to think of options?
Because creativity and imagination are brain functions which are impaired by stress. The more pressure you are under, the less able the brain is to use its creative part. Remember, thinking of options is not making a decision or a commitment – that comes later.

Surely this all takes a lot of time?
Yes. But no one is suggesting you waste time unnecessarily. For simple decisions, you might not need to find out any information, you might only have a few options, or you might be able to work out the answer more or less straight away. Use the method in this chapter for longer, more complicated, 'messy' situations, to clarify your ideas and help you justify your decisions.

EVALUATING OPTIONS AND MAKING DECISIONS

Looking at advantages and disadvantages
The simplest way of evaluating the options is to look at the advantages and disadvantages (or pros and cons) of each, and also the likely results of implementing them. For

Table 1. Looking at options			
Option	*Advantage*	*Disadvantages*	*Likely results*
1. Reduce workload	Reduces time pressure	Less work done. Staff may get of it! bored	More accurate work but less
2. Train staff	Increases work accuracy, Staff able to cope with time pressures	Takes time. May cost	Increased accuracy
3. Give incentives or bonus schemes	Improved staff morale and motivation	Costs money. May demotivate those unable to achieve bonuses	May improve accuracy, but cause conflict
4. Introduce accuracy checks	Will 'weed out' inaccurate work	Takes time. May antagonise staff. Won't improve work, just remove substandard work	Increased accuracy, but decreased amount of work done

example, using our previous example of how to improve accuracy, the problems were lack of time and low staff motivation. Let's imagine the main options were:

1. reduce workload
2. train staff to work faster and more accurately
3. give incentive or bonus schemes
4. introduce accuracy checks.

54

Table 2. Considering constraints

Option	No money available	Workload must be maintained	Staff must feel happy
1.	✓	X	✓
2.	X	✓ after training period	✓
3.	X	✓	?
4.	✓	X	?

Make a chart and fill in the advantages, disadvantages and likely results for each. Table 1 shows this.

From Table 1, we can see that option (2) is obviously likely to produce the best result. However, you do need to check whether you have any *constraints* on your decision. This option will possibly cost money. If none is available, the option can be discounted. It will also take time, and if none can be allowed, again, you need to find another option.

Considering constraints

A further idea is to add columns to the right-hand side of the chart, showing any constraints, and tick or cross to indicate whether they apply to that option. You tick options that are not affected, and cross options that would break the constraint.

An example of this can be seen in Table 2. From this we can see that now, we have no ideal option: option (2) would be best if there was money available, otherwise no option completely solves the problem within the given constraints.

You would have to remove one of the constraints (e.g. allocate some money, or agree to a temporary reduction in workload), or go back and think of some more options. This need not be a problem: one of the main things that people worry about is getting the right answer. Well, there may not be a *right* answer, just a *best* answer.

Your best answer may be a combination of two or more options. In the above example, how about combining options (3) and (4)? Organise a competition among staff for the highest rate of accurate work. This is based on option (3), but involves a competition rather than a bonus or incentive scheme. Monitor accuracy (option (4)), and from the results, award the winner a prize – perhaps a half-day off, or a bottle of wine, or some other incentive that need not cost a great deal. You could award a badge or trophy.

A variation of this would be to use teams of staff in competition with each other. This would have an advantage, as even staff with no chance of winning on an individual basis could still win as part of a team – it motivates everybody.

Can you think of any other possibilities?

Using priorities

If you have difficulty deciding, especially where you have several options that would work, try using some priorities. Let's imagine that all the four options in our example were possible, and all would produce the desired effect. To decide which is the best one, look at what priorities you have, and which order they rank in.

Common priorities would include:

- time

- cost

- equipment

- staff morale/motivation

- meeting targets and deadlines.

Table 3. Using weighting

Option	Cost	Time	Staff	Achieving targets	Total
(1)	2	4	2	4	12
(2)	4	2	1	1	8
(3)	3	1	3	2	9
(4)	1	3	4	3	11

Which is the most important? Decide on an order of priority, and see which option is the best, bearing in mind the priorities. This method is very useful when you don't have any constraints to limit your options.

Using weighting
An alternative method is to weight, or score options. You score each option against criteria that are important, which you choose. Score one for the best option, and so on. Options which tie are simply given the same score. Add up the points, and the option with the least points wins! Table 3 shows an example of this.

From Table 3, you can see that the best option by far would be option (2), without the constraints we applied earlier. So what would you do, if the lack of available funds really was a constraint? Simply cross the option off the list and don't even consider it in your weighting chart, because it really isn't practical. So only put options which are practical in your weighting chart.

This method is especially good for making open decisions such as buying equipment – which model to buy. Simply list the criteria you would like, then score the options, add up the scores, and see which item best fits your requirements.

Table 4. Weighting system to decide which computer to purchase

Computer

Model	A	B	C	D	E	F
Easy to use	1	2	3	5	4	6
Long guarantee	2	1	4	3	6	5
Compatible with existing equipment	4	5	2	1	6	3
Reasonable cost	1	6	2	5	4	3
Large memory	1	2	6	3	5	4
Speed of operation	1	4	5	6	2	3
Total	10	20	22	23	27	24

An example of using the weighting system to decide which model of computer to purchase is shown in Table 4. Model A is the clear winner, and what is more, you know your decision was *objective* – you weren't persuaded by the salesman's talk, by how the machine looks, or a friend's recommendation – all your judgement was based on was factual criteria. Such judgements and decisions are easy to justify and explain to people, even if the decision is contentious.

CASE STUDY

Bev fails to evaluate options
The care assistants are due to have new uniforms, and Matron asks Bev to choose the design. Bev gets the

brochures, and asks everyone what they think. She takes a vote, and puts the first two choices to Matron. The first choice is too expensive, so Matron goes ahead and orders the second choice. When the new uniforms come, they are 'dry clean only', and can't be issued to staff. The exercise has to be done again, and this time Matron chooses. Bev feels very silly.

Bev should have evaluated the options fully, not simply trusted people to choose sensibly. What she didn't do was to use factual criteria to evaluate the choices available. She could have included constraints, such as giving people a free choice but stipulating that choices had to be washable.

IMPLEMENTING, FOLLOWING UP, EVALUATING

So that's it – you've made your decision. But don't stop there: you now need to tie up all the loose ends.

Recording
- Keep a written record of any information gathered, and options you came up with. If the decision needs to be looked at again, you don't have to 'reinvent the wheel'.

Communicating
- Tell people what you decided, explain why, and let people know how you intend to carry it out. Talking to people face-to-face is best, because you can gauge people's reactions, and 'sell' them the decision if necessary.

- Make sure *everybody* knows – your own boss, other managers and your own staff.

- Ask people how things are going when the decision is in progress. Just because things are working, it doesn't necessarily mean that difficulties are not being experienced.

- If your decision works, thank everyone that helped you with it.

Monitoring and evaluating

- Once the decision is in force, monitor how things go. Check that the expected result actually occurs. If not, you may have to look at the issue again.

- Don't be afraid to make adjustments to your decision if necessary. It doesn't mean you 'got it wrong' if these are necessary, it just means your idea needs refining.

- Check for new problems in other areas that your decision may cause – often changing one thing has a 'knock-on' effect. Again, it doesn't mean your decision is wrong, it just means you now have some other issues to work on.

- If your decision doesn't work, learn from it.

MANAGEMENT TIPS

- Don't be afraid to ask for help, information, advice or especially ideas.

- Don't put off unpleasant decisions, or when you come to make them, you will be rushed and therefore less able to think creatively.

- Don't keep 'reinventing the wheel' – solving the same problem again and again. If this is happening, you aren't solving it properly!

- Don't be afraid to use intuition. If you have no clear 'best' option, use your intuition – play a 'hunch', follow your 'gut feeling' or 'sixth sense'. These are all names for imaginative, creative thinking.

ACTION POINTS

1. What is the most important decision you have made at work recently? Could the methods in this chapter have helped? Would you have come to the same decision using them?

2. Think of an example where you or someone else made a wrong or bad decision. Apply the methods in this chapter to see what better decision could have been arrived at.

3. Think of a problem you have to solve. What is the real problem? What do you want to achieve – the ideal solution? Now apply the techniques in this chapter to solving it.

4

Managing Resources

MANAGING TECHNOLOGY

Technology can be intimidating, but a basic appreciation of what is available and how it works will help you understand how you can make best use of it at work.

Understanding computers

Computers handle masses of data and information at high speed. Three types of computer are common: mainframes, microcomputers and portable computers.

Mainframe
These have a huge information processing capacity, and are large systems which are used via a **terminal**. A terminal is simply a screen (called a visual display unit – a VDU – or monitor) and a keyboard, connected electronically to the mainframe, or central computer. The mainframe itself can be many miles away, and usually needs an air-conditioned room to protect it from things like dirt, dust and humidity.

Microcomputers
These are often called personal computers or PCs. They are smaller, and consist of a screen and keyboard, the computer processor itself, and usually a disk drive for recording and reading information on computer disks.

Portable computers
These are often called laptops or notebooks, because they are so small. They have the features and capabilities of PCs in a portable form.

Networking
Computers are often linked electronically to form a network. This means that the linked computers can communicate electronically with each other. The advantage of this is that information can be accessed by any computer in the network.

Modems
A modem connects a computer to others through the telephone system. This allows you to transmit and receive information. While the modem is connected, you are part of the network, but the connection is broken when the modem is disconnected. The **Internet,** an international information network, may be accessed by modem, and many people use this to access information.

Scanners
Scanners read printed or drawn material from a page into a computer. With them, you can input pictures, maps, diagrams etc into the computer.

E-mail
E-mail is electronic mail. It is simply sending and receiving electronic information over a network or modem, rather than on paper.

Appreciating modern telecommunications
Telephones have been in use for very many years. Technology is changing our telecommunications, however, with new improved devices and systems, to save time and make life easier.

Voice-mail
Voice-mail systems use a computer as well as a telephone system. They are similar to an answerphone, taking messages, but can do much more, giving you far more options. They are usually operated by pressing code keys on your telephone, and so you need a 'tone phone' to use them. This is a telephone that 'beeps' when you press the

keys – the sound tells the computer what to do, just like pressing a key on a computer keyboard. Voicemail systems are already in use for telephone banking and for queuing systems, and more applications are being developed all the time.

Call forwarding
This means you can programme your phone to automatically forward all your calls to another phone.

Conference calls
The operator can connect several people to the same telephone conversation. This allows several people to take part in a conversation at once.

It is worth asking your operator what facilities you can use on your telephone, as they will be able to keep you up-to-date with all the latest developments.

MANAGING STOCK

Stock can mean many things. We often talk about **consumables**, which are materials and supplies which are frequently used and therefore need replacing often, such as paper, pens, envelopes, scissors etc.

Stock can also mean warehouse goods. Non-consumable items are usually called **capital items**, as this sort of stock forms part of the capital or worth of the organisation.

Stock control

Good stock control keeps costs down, while keeping enough stock available. It involves receiving stock, storing and checking (auditing) it, ordering it, and issuing it. Some organisations have manual systems to keep track of stock, while others use a computer system.

It does not matter whether you are dealing with a warehouse full of capital items or a cupboard full of

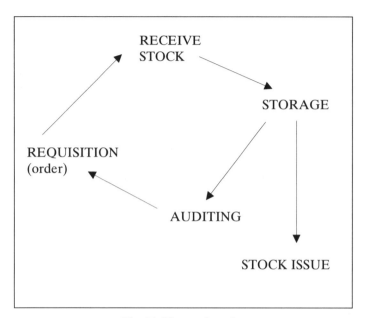

Fig. 11. The stock cycle.

stationery – the principles of good stock control are the same.

Fig. 11 shows the stock cycle.

Receiving stock
Check goods received carefully for damaged, incomplete or missing items. Do not rely on delivery notes – unpack goods, count and check them yourself. If there are any problems, inform the supplier immediately. You can also take the following steps.

Damaged items
Check before you sign for the items whether you are signing to say they are in good condition. If so, do not sign, or write the details of the damage on the delivery note before signing it.

Missing items
Check the delivery note for items marked 'out of stock', 'to follow' or 'discontinued'. 'Out of stock' means there are no supplies, and you need to reorder. 'To follow' means they will be sent separately later (keep a note of this and check they do arrive). 'Discontinued' means the item is no longer available. Some suppliers automatically send a replacement for these, but legally you do not have to accept replacement items if they are not suitable. Do not sign for the items unless the discrepancies are clearly shown on the delivery note.

Incorrect or additional items
These goods should be returned. Ensure your organisation does not pay for them.

CASE STUDY

Bev's assistant fails to check a delivery
When the new staff uniforms arrive, it is late, and Bev is busy. A new girl, Lucy, is asked to sign for them so the delivery man doesn't have to wait. But when they are unpacked, there are 2 missing. The company is called, but they say the correct number were dispatched. Lucy gets into trouble because she hadn't checked the delivery.

Bev usually checks all deliveries herself, and is right to do so. Had she checked this one, she would have counted the uniforms and the problem wouldn't have arisen. She should have asked Lucy to sign for the delivery, but made sure she knew how to check it before doing so, or got somebody else to do it for her.

Storing stock
- Guard against theft.

- Keep a proper record of exactly what stock you have.

- Keep faster moving items where they are most easily accessible.

- Keep large bulky items low down to avoid heavy lifting.

- Know which items are *active* and which are *inactive*. Active items are frequently used and need a high level of stock available. Inactive items are less frequently used, and need only a low level of stock.

- Label all stock clearly.

- Store hazardous items safely and legally.

- Store stock carefully to prevent waste and damage.

- Store stock with labels facing upwards and outwards, so they can easily be read.

- Undertake regular checks to see if stocks of any item are running low.

- Use stock in rotation, so items do not get left in stock for long periods of time. Rotation means always issuing your oldest stock and keeping the newest. This ensures your stock does not get outdated. Place new stock under or behind old stock to ensure this.

Auditing stock

- Carry out a regular stock check or inventory, by counting stock against the recorded levels.

- Investigate any discrepancies carefully.

- Adjust the stock record to take account of any unusable stock, so it can be disposed of. Examples of this would be stock damaged beyond use, which is obsolete, or out of date.

Issuing stock

- Only issue stock to authorised people.

- Monitor excessive requests for stock or short-notice urgent demands – perhaps these could be avoided by better planning.

Ordering stock

- Order stock in good time – remembering there will probably be a delivery time. Stock does not magically appear as soon as you order it.

- When you order stock, remember you will probably have used up some more of the item before the new delivery arrives. You might therefore want to order more than required, to compensate for this.

- Be aware of any maximum stock levels set. These are important, as holding stock ties up money (working capital) which might be needed elsewhere in the organisation.

CASE STUDY

Nikki learns about stock security

Nikki doesn't bother to keep the office stationery locked away. 'People need to be able to get things as and when they need them in a busy office,' she was told when she took over. After five months, she orders some more notebooks and computer disks, only to find that her budget allocation has all been spent. When she looks into it, the quantities that have been used are ridiculous. Obviously, somebody is dishonest, but who?

Nikki realises that too many people have access to the office, including after her team have gone home. To keep her stock safe and secure, she needs to at least lock things away at the end of the day. Regular checks would have brought the problem to light long before it was this extensive.

QUESTIONS AND ANSWERS

We have computers and word processors at work, but I've never used one. Does it matter?
Not unless you need to use one for your job. However,

they are nothing to be afraid of. Most adult education
centres do evening classes in computing, and you could
learn more that way. At work, it would be useful if you
made sure you were aware of what the computers do –
what information they handle and what jobs they do. You
can't make effective use of them as a resource unless you
understand their capabilities.

*We regularly run out of some items. Where am I going
wrong?*
In one of two ways. Perhaps you don't keep enough of
these items in stock, so you need to order larger quantities
and stock up. Alternatively, perhaps you are ordering
enough, but because it takes a long time for the new stock
to be delivered, you run out before the new supply arrives.
If this is the case, order earlier – set a level, and as soon as
stock gets down to that level, reorder. Once you have
found the right level you should have no more problems.

MANAGING MONEY – PETTY CASH AND INVOICES

Petty cash
Petty cash is money kept to cover small items of day-to-day
expenditure. The amount held varies, depending on how
long the money is supposed to last – normally one week or
one month. The amount held may sometimes be called an
imprest account.

Why use cash?
• For emergency purchases, e.g. special postage.

• To pay people who only accept cash, e.g. the milkman,
  or office window cleaner.

• To pay for purchases too small to warrant an invoice or
  cheque.

Checking petty cash
• Check that expenditure is only for authorised payments.

- Check that expenditure is recorded accurately and substantiated by a receipt or voucher.

- Check the cash is secure at all times.

- Check that the amount held is exactly the amount that should be left, after deducting receipts and vouchers.

Using vouchers and receipts

Some organisations pay people from petty cash in return for a receipt. Other organisations use petty cash vouchers – these are an authority to spend money, and should ideally have a receipt attached. You need receipts or vouchers to balance the petty cash – simply add up amounts on the receipts and vouchers paid, and this is the total paid out. Subtract this from the petty cash total, and the remainder should be what you have in cash.

Replacing petty cash

When the petty cash runs low, it needs to be replaced by Accounts or the appropriate person. You add up the expenditure in categories, and total how much has been spent. This can then be replaced, so you have a full amount of petty cash again.

If the petty cash runs out before the end of the week or month regularly, consider asking for an increase in the amount held. This will save you time and work.

Checking invoices and invoice terms

The following is a list of things you may see on an invoice, and gives some advice on how to check them.

Carrier forward
This means the buyer is liable to pay the delivery charges.

Carriage paid
This means the supplier will pay the delivery charges. Check that delivery charges do not get added to the invoice.

Cash discount
This is a discount given for prompt payment. Terms should be quoted on the invoice. Check the discount is deducted and is the right amount.

Credit note
This is a note sent because a previous invoice charged too much. This may be because goods were overcharged, goods were returned, or fewer goods were delivered than on the invoice. If you are expecting a credit note, you must monitor carefully that it arrives and that it is for the correct amount.

Debit note
This is a supplementary invoice. It means that the original invoice did not include all the charges. It is usually because goods were undercharged, too many goods were sent, more expensive goods were sent, or an item was omitted from the original invoice. Check these invoices carefully to be sure the charges have not been previously paid.

Delivery address
Check it is the right address.

Delivery charges
Check that you should be paying these and not the supplier. Check that they are at the correct rate.

Description/reference number
Check that the item(s) are what was ordered.

Discount
Check that the rate of discount quoted is correct and that the discount has been calculated correctly.

Dispatch date
Check the goods have been dispatched, i.e. check that the date is in the past. Check against a delivery note or goods received note that they have been received.

Errors and omissions excepted
Invoices often say 'E&OE', which mean errors and omissions excepted. This means that if there are any items missed off, or any mistakes have been made, the supplier retains the right to send you a supplementary invoice.

Name
Check the invoice carries your name and/or the right organisation's name. Otherwise, it may cause accounting or auditing problems.

Order number
Check against the order that the order bears the correct number – this means the order was authorised and ordered officially.

Price
Check the order or the quotation to ensure the price is correct.

Quantity
Check that the quantity quoted is both what was ordered and what was received.

Statement
This is a statement of the account, and should list all invoices, payments made and credits, and an overall balance. They are usually issued monthly, like a bank statement. They need to be carefully checked.

Supplementary invoices
These are also called debit notes (see above).

Terms for payment
Check that these are as agreed, and that you are paying within the agreed time.

Total price
Check the calculations have been added up correctly.

Trade discount
This is a discount given as an allowance if large orders are placed, or if the supplier is in the same trade as your organisation. Check that the discount is deducted.

VAT rate
Check that the VAT rate is correct, and that the amount of VAT has been calculated correctly.

CASE STUDY

Mike checks the petty cash

Mike's section uses petty cash for purchases of coffee, tea etc, for which they have an imprest account of £100 per month. Tom looks after this, but Mike starts to notice that Tom asks for a 'top up' of cash almost every month. On investigation, Mike finds that other sections are all coming to Tom for petty cash – for taxis, parking tickets, emergency stationery supplies etc.

The amount of Tom's time this petty cash account is taking is ridiculous – no wonder his work often seems rushed. Mike needs to tell others that this account is for his team's use only. Poor Tom – he has been giving out cash for things he isn't really authorised to, and also making himself a lot of work in the process.

MANAGEMENT TIPS

- Find out what technology is available in your workplace, and what it can do.

- Keep careful stock control – audit regularly, and keep good records.

- Be alert for discrepancies when receiving stock.

- Store stock well, so it is safe, secure and easy to handle.

- Order stock carefully, and check all invoices, delivery notes and other paperwork.

- Always keep accurate accounts of petty cash.

ACTION POINTS

1. What stock do you control? Is it properly recorded and accounted for? How could you improve your stock handling?

2. Do you check invoices correctly? What procedures do you have for making sure that errors are corrected and accounted for?

5

Managing Standards

As managers, we all have certain legal obligations. The law gives employees rights, and places obligations and responsibilities on employers and managers. This chapter is intended to give you an insight into three main areas of your legal responsibility – health and safety, data protection and employment law.

MANAGING HEALTH AND SAFETY AT WORK

Health and safety at work is everyone's responsibility. However, as a manager, you can be held personally responsible for health and safety – responsible for ensuring that your organisation operates safely and with due regard for health. You have a second responsibility to do whatever is *reasonably practicable* to achieve this. This phrase effectively means that the degree of risk in a particular job or place of work needs to be balanced against the time, trouble, physical difficulty and cost of taking measures to avoid or reduce the risk.

Understanding the Health and Safety at Work Act 1974
The Act had four main aims:

- To ensure the health, safety and welfare of people at work, by giving responsibility for it to everybody – employees, supervisors and managers.

- To protect non-employees from risks to their health or safety which might come from employees and their work.

- To control storage and use of explosive, flammable or

dangerous substances, and to prevent such substances being obtained, possessed or used unless a person is legally entitled to do so.

- To control emissions of noxious or poisonous substances into the atmosphere.

What did the Act do?
- It brought the law on health, safety and welfare at work up to date.

- It created a Health and Safety Commission, which has inspectors to give advice and to enforce the regulations.

- It created a range of duties which employers had to carry out.

- It reorganised the various existing government inspectors.

- It gave new powers and penalties to enforce safety laws.

- It established new accident prevention measures.

Knowing your responsibilities under the Act
The Act details the duties of employers, employees and non-employees. These duties are important to us as managers, as we need to carry them out to comply with the law. As managers, we are employers under the Act, although we are also employees – so we have twice as many duties as non-managers!

Understanding the duties of employers to employees
Section 2 of the Act covers the duties of employers to employees. The main duties are as follows:

- You have a duty to ensure so far as is reasonably practicable, the health, safety and welfare at work of employees.

- You have a duty to provide and maintain **plant**

(machinery equipment and appliances used at work) that is safe and without health risks.

- You have a duty to ensure that everything used at work and all work activities are safe and without health risk. This especially refers to handling, transport and storage of materials and substances.

- You have a duty to provide information, instruction, training and supervision, so employees are safe and without health risk at work.

- You have a duty to maintain any place of work under your control in a safe and health risk-free condition. You also have a duty to provide facilities, entrances, exits and arrangements for welfare at work that are safe and free from health risk.

- You have a duty to prepare and revise a written health and safety policy statement. You also have a duty to bring this to the attention of all employees.

Understanding the duties of employers to non-employees

- You have a responsibility to protect non-employees, such as members of the public, at your place of work.

- You have a duty to carry out business in such a way that non-employees who may be affected by the business are not exposed to risks to their health or safety.

- You have a duty to give non-employees information about things that may affect their health or safety.

Understanding other duties of employers

In addition to all the above, employers also have certain special duties, which apply if you are in charge of premises or if you:

- design

- manufacture

- import

- supply

- erect or

- install

any article, machinery, equipment, substance or appliance for use at work.

Understanding the duties of employees

All employees, including managers, have three main duties:

1. You have a duty to take reasonable care of your own health and safety, and that of others who may be affected by the things you do, or do not do, at work.

2. You have a duty to co-operate with your employer as far as necessary, to enable them to carry out their own duties and requirements.

3. You have a duty not to intentionally or recklessly misuse or interfere with anything provided for health, safety or welfare purposes.

What happens when things go wrong?

Inspectors
Inspectors have the following powers:

- To enter any premises at a reasonable time.

- To bring an authorised person with them.

- To take samples, measurements, photographs and recordings.

- To require people to provide information, to answer questions, and to sign a declaration of truth.

78

When an inspector feels that health and safety needs enforcing, they have the power to do two things:

1. *Improvement notices* – an organisation is 'served with' (given) an improvement notice if an inspector thinks that the law has been contravened. An improvement notice gives the details, and asks the employer to put the situation right within a specified amount of time.

2. *Prohibition notices* – an organisation is served with a prohibition notice if an inspector thinks there is a risk of serious personal injury. A prohibition notice means that work must stop immediately. If the inspector thinks the risk is not imminent, they may issue a **deferred** prohibition notice. This means that work must stop if matters are not put right within a certain period of time.

Penalties
If you do not comply with an improvement notice, a prohibition notice or deferred prohibition notice, you may be taken to court and fined or imprisoned.

Other information/legislation
The Health and Safety at Work Act is the basis of British health and safety law, and is called an **enabling** act. This means it is general in nature and covers a broad range of situations and issues. It is an Act through which further legislation can be (and has been) added. Where the Health and Safety Commission and/or Executive (HSE) consider action is necessary to supplement the current legislation and information, they have three main choices:

- Guidance
- Approved Codes of Practice
- Regulations.

Guidance
Guidance is not compulsory, and employers are free to

take other action. But following guidance is normally enough to comply with the law. The HSE publishes guidance on a range of subjects to:

- interpret and help people understand what the law says
- help people comply with the law
- give technical advice.

Approved Codes of Practice
These have a special legal status. They are not compulsory, but if an employer is prosecuted for a breach of health and safety law and they did not follow the Approved Code of Practice, a court can find them at fault unless they can show they complied with the law in some other way.

Regulations
These are law, approved by Parliament.

The Management of Health and Safety at Work Regulations 1992

These regulations came into effect on 1 January 1993, under the provisions of the Health and Safety at Work Act 1974. They extend the employer's general safety obligations of the 1974 Act. The main requirement of employers is to carry out a *risk assessment*. Employers with five or more employees need to record the significant findings of the assessment.

Employers also need to:

- make arrangements for implementing health and safety measures indentified by the risk assessment
- appoint competent people to help them implement the measures
- set up emergency procedures
- provide clear information and training to employees

- work together with other employers sharing the same workplace.

Reporting of Injuries, Diseases and Dangerous Occurrences Regulations (RIDDOR) 1985

These regulations require you to report certain incidents to the Health and Safety Executive, or to the environmental health department of your local authority. Failing to do this is a criminal offence. The Regulations were made so that trends in incidents could be seen on a national basis, and advice given as to how to avoid common incidents.

What to report
1. You must immediately report, by telephone:
- any fatal or major injuries to anybody in an accident connected with your business

- any dangerous occurrences listed in the regulations.

2. You must also report in writing and within seven days:
- any of the above

- any other injury to an employee which results in them being away from work or unable to do their normal work for more than three days (including weekends and days off)

- any cases of ill health listed in the Regulations.

Record-keeping
You must keep a record of anything you need to report. This record must include the date, time, place, personal details and a brief description of the event.

Checklist of good practice for managers
- Allocate responsibility to people for health and safety.

- Carry out a regular inspection of the workplace, looking for hazards and risks.

- Check adequate first aid facilities are available.

- Check safe working practices and methods are in use.

- Ensure employees are trained in health and safety.

- Ensure all health and safety measures under your responsibility are carried out.

- Give employees a written health and safety policy.

- Carry out induction for new employees, so they know about health and safety.

- Issue and regularly check safety equipment and protective clothing. Also ensure that this is used or worn whenever necessary.

- Liase with superiors about health and safety.

- Make sure that you have proper procedures for working that are safe, to prevent accidents. These should be in writing if possible.

- Provide appropriate fire-fighting equipment, and make sure that fire drills are carried out regularly.

- Remind employees regularly about health and safety.

- Report accidents, near misses and hazards.

- Set up a safety group or committee, or make sure employees know how to make suggestions and bring things to your attention about health and safety.

- Carry out regular assessments of risk.

CASE STUDY

Bev fails to prevent an accident

Bev notices a piece of frayed carpet, and makes a mental note to put up a sign. But with everything else going on, she forgets. The next day, Shiela trips on the carpet and Bev remembers to put up a warning sign. A few days later, another care assistant catches her foot on the carpet and falls with a tray of hot tea. Bev blames herself, and Matron is furious. 'Why didn't you put a note in the accident book, so the caretaker could see there was a problem and fix it?' she stormed. 'This could have been a lot more serious, you know.'

Bev should definitely have put up a notice straight away, or blocked off the area. Then she should have recorded it in the accident book so the caretaker knew of the problem. But then again, who is her Health and Safety rep? Matron isn't entirely fair in blaming Bev, who had clearly not been trained in Health and Safety procedures.

PROTECTING COMPUTER DATA

Information is held about everybody on computer – from the day we are born, computers collect and store information about us and our identity. Computer records have many advantages – they are faster and more efficient than looking up information manually. However, there are potential problems with having information stored about you on a computer and the Data Protection Act 1998 was introduced to set standards for accuracy and use of computer data. It came into force on 1 March 2000.

What does the Act cover?
The Act covers 'Personal Data', which is:

- automatically processed information (which usually means processed by a computer)

- certain manual records, depending on how they are structured and accessed

- about living, identifiable individuals.

How does the Act work?
The Act gives rights to individuals, and sets responsibilities for data users to be open about the use to which they put personal data, and to follow sound and proper practices.

What are an individual's rights?

- To see information about themselves held on a computer or otherwise under the Act.

- To complain about the misuse of your information.

- To object to lawful processing.

- To have information about how automated decisions are reached.

- To have judicial remedy for breaches of rights and compensation for breaches of law.

- To seek redress through the Data Protection Commissioner or directly through the courts.

What are the Data User's responsibilities?

Data Users must register with the Data Protection Registrar (with few exceptions). They must then comply with the Data Protection principles of good information handling practice. These require that data must be:

- Obtained and processed fairly and lawfully.

- Held for the lawful purposes described in the Data User's registration.

- Used for those purposes, and disclosed to those people only as detailed in the Register.

- Adequate, relevant and not excessive in relation to the purpose for which the data is held.

- Accurate and up-to-date where necessary.

- Held no longer than is necessary for the registered purpose.

- Accessible to the individual concerned, who has the right to have information erased or corrected where appropriate.

- Surrounded by the proper security.

How do you register?
Contact the Registrar's Office. There is a fee to cover registration for a certain period of time.

CASE STUDY

Nikki omits to follow Data Protection rules
Nikki's predecessor left a file on her computer, containing the details of all the office staff and notes on their performance. Nikki had never used such a thing before, but as it was on the computer, and needed Nikki's password to access it, she began to find it useful to note comments on people every now and then, mainly to remind her of things to include in their annual appraisals. One day when tidying up the department computer server, Peter found this file, but obviously couldn't open it. Nikki explains, and Peter is very offended that records about him and others are being kept on the computer.

Nikki doesn't see that this is any different from making a note on someone's personnel file. But as this file has never been registered for Data Protection purposes, and contains confidential information, she is actually doing something she shouldn't. Potentially, she could be in trouble, unless she reports it to her Data Protection Officer immediately.

QUESTIONS AND ANSWERS

This all sounds very technical and complicated. Where can I get more information?
Further information about health and safety, including a wide range of leaflets, can be obtained from:

The Health and Safety Executive Information Centre
Broad Lane
Sheffield
S3 7HQ

For further information about data protection, contact:

The Office of the Data Protection Registrar
Wycliffe House
Water Lane
Wilmslow
Cheshire
SK9 5AF

What are the consequences if I don't carry out all my duties?
Ultimately, you may end up in court – not to obey one of
these Acts is committing a criminal offence. You can be
prosecuted and fined in court, or even imprisoned.

UNDERSTANDING EMPLOYMENT LAW

The law gives employees certain rights. These **statutory
rights** apply to part-time as well as full-time workers, and
even **homeworkers** so long as they are employees. Some
rights are applicable to **workers**, a term which may include
contractors, temporary workers or casual workers.

As an employer, you must observe people's statutory
rights, or you are in breach of the law, and you can be
penalised. The main way of doing this is by an **industrial
tribunal**. Employers can be more generous than the
minimum requirements, and if they are, the better rights
are usually stipulated in some form of contract. Employers
cannot put into a contract things which are *less* beneficial
than the statutory rights.

Some rights have a **qualifying period** or minimum period
of time a worker or employee has to have worked to be
entitled to them. Some rights list **exemptions** – categories
of worker or employee who are not covered by them. This
chapter lists a large number of rights – some people will be
exempt or will not have worked the minimum qualifying
period. *You will need to check the relevant legislation in
detail to find out all the exact qualifying periods and
exemptions.*

Working time

- Workers should not be required to work more than 48 hours each week unless they agree to do so in writing.

- Workers are entitled to 11 hours rest in each 24 hours. Under 18s are entitled to 12 hours.

- Workers are entitled to a break from work of 20 minutes if they work more than 6 hours a day (under 18s a break of 30 minutes). This is over and above the daily rest breaks above.

- Night workers should not be required to work more than an average of 8 hours in every 24. Where night work is strenuous or hazardous, 8 hours in 24 is the maximum a night worker may work.

- Workers are entitled to a minimum of one day's rest each week, or two days every two weeks. Under 18s are entitled to two days rest each week.

- Workers are eligible for entitlement to paid annual leave.

Pay

- Employees are entitled to a minimum wage as detailed in the relevant legislation.

- Employees have the right to pay when they would normally expect to work but no work is available. This means if people are laid off for a whole day or days, they have the right to pay.

- Employees have the right to an itemised statement of pay at the time of payment. This must detail gross earnings, net pay and fixed and variable deductions.

- If their employer becomes insolvent, an employee has the right to wages and other payment rights as if they were wages under the Bankruptcy Acts and Companies Acts.

- Employees have the right to information about their occupational pension schemes.

Maternity/Parental leave
- Pregnant employees have the right to maternity leave, and the right to return to their old job after giving birth.

- Employees have the right to basic employment conditions under their employment contract during maternity absence.

- Women have the right to maternity pay.

- Women have the right to a written reason for dismissal, if dismissed whilst pregnant or on maternity leave.

- Pregnant women have the right to paid time off for ante-natal care.

- Employees may have the right to parental leave.

Periods of notice
- Employees have the right to notice after one month's service.

- Employees who are given notice have the right to be paid during the notice period, whether or not they are able to work.

Disability
- People with disabilities have the right not to be discriminated against in employment or training.

Sickness
- Employees have the right to full pay if they are suspended from work on medical grounds for certain conditions.

- Employees have the right to Statutory Sick Pay for absences of four days or more.

- Employees have the right to withhold consent, so the

employer cannot insist on a medical report from an employee's own doctor.

- Employees have the right to have access to any medical report, before it goes to their employer. They also have the right to comment on that report, or to refuse consent to it being passed to their employer, or to request incorrect or misleading parts of the report to be corrected.

Time off
- Employees have the right to have time off (unpaid) to fulfil duties as a:
  —justice of the peace
  —local councillor
  —member of a statutory tribunal
  —member of a regional or area health authority
  —governor or manager of a state school
  —member of the Environmental Protection Agency
  —member of Boards of Visitors in England, Wales or Scotland
  —member of Visiting Committees to prisons, remand centres and young offender institutions.

- Employees who are made redundant have the right to reasonable paid time off to look for a new job, or to arrange training for a new job.

- Employees have the right to take unpaid leave to carry out reserve military duties.

- Employees who are called up to military service have the right to return to employment afterwards.

Health and safety
- Employees have the right to a healthy and safe working environment.

- Members of recognised Trade Unions have the right to ask the company to set up a safety committee, on which they may be represented.

Trade unions

- Employees have the right to belong to an independent trade union of their choice.

- Employees have the right to refuse to belong to a staff association that is not independent (i.e. one that is subject to interference by the company).

- Employees have the right to be accompanied (but not represented) by a fellow employee or trade union representative in grievance and disciplinary procedures.

Infringement of rights

- Employees dismissed for trying to obtain their statutory rights have the right to complain to an industrial tribunal.

The main Acts and Regulations relevant in Employment Law

Access to Medical Records Act 1988
Access to Medical Records Act 1990
Asylum and Immigration Act 1996
Companies Act 1985
Data Protection Act 1984 and 1998
Disability Discrimination Act 1999
Employment Act 1980
Employment Act 1988
Employment Act 1989
Employment Act 1990
Employment Protection (Consolidation) Act 1978
Employment Protection (Part-Time) Employees Regulations 1995
Employment Relations Act 1999
Factories Act 1961
Health and Safety at Work Act 1974
Maternity (Compulsory Leave) Regulations 1994
Offices, Shops and Railway Premises Act 1963
Police Act 1997
Rehabilitation of Offenders Act 1974
Reserve Forces (Safeguard of Employment) Act 1985

Sex Discrimination Act 1975
Sex Discrimination Act 1986
Social Services Contributions and Benefits Act 1992
Trade Union and Labour Relations (Consolidation) Act
1992
Trade Union Reform and Employment Rights Act 1993
TUPE – Transfer of Undertakings (Protection of
Employment) Regulations 1981
Wages Act 1986
Working Time Regulations (SI 1998 No 1833)

CASE STUDY

Mike learns about maternity rights

Rachel tells Mike she is expecting a baby, and after a few
months she starts to suffer some morning sickness. She is
occasionally late in due to this, and her work begins to pile
up. When she asks Mike for time off for ante-natal classes,
he explodes. 'What? Rachel, you're hardly here as it is!
You're an excellent worker, but your work's getting so far
behind we all have to help out. I don't mind you going, but
you'll just have to make up the work, or take work home
with you.' Rachel complains to Personnel, and the HR
Manager is not pleased.

Mike doesn't know his employment law – pregnant
employees have the right to time off for antenatal classes,
as the HR Manager points out. Mike, like most managers,
isn't an expert, so he should have checked carefully before
saying anything. He should know to take advice from
people who specialise in such things before making
decisions.

MANAGEMENT TIPS

- Be aware of your responsibilities for health and safety,
  data protection and employment law.

- Know what your organisation's policies and procedures are regarding these three areas.

- Query anything you are not sure about.

- Get specialist advice or information in the relevant legislation whenever necessary.

ACTION POINTS

1. Ensure that you have a copy of your organisation's health and safety policy and that all your staff know about it. Are they trained to work safely in everything they do?

2. What data do you hold on computer? Is it registered with the Data Protection Registrar? If not, does it need to be?

3. Do you know where to get advice on employment issues, for example from Personnel/Human Resources? Do you know what your responsibilities for staff are?

6

Managing Meetings

MAKING MEETINGS SUCCESSFUL

Meetings can be a nightmare. However, there is a formula for successful meetings, and following it should guarantee you better meetings, whether you are running them (called 'chairing' them) or just attending. One of the keys lies in knowing that there are two results you want from a meeting – satisfaction and achievement of business.

A meeting can be successful in achieving its business, but if that is done in a way that leaves those present feeling dissatisfied, they are less likely to co-operate next time. Conversely, an enjoyable meeting is not necessarily successful, unless it also achieves its business.

The formula for a successful meeting can be found in Fig. 12.

AGENDA   + PARTICIPATION = RESULTS

- realistic

- purposeful
  – to inform
  – to consult
  – to decide

- introduction

- motivation

- listening

- control

- summary

- satisfaction

- achievement
  of business

Fig. 12. Formula for a successful meeting.

CASE STUDY

Mike's team meeting leaves the members dissatisfied

Mike goes to a team meeting for the first time. Just before
the meeting begins, the chairperson calls him, to explain
she can't make it. 'Can you chair for me?' she asks. 'I'd be
really grateful, and I don't want to cancel it.' Mike agrees,
and runs the meeting very efficiently. It takes about three
quarters of an hour, compared with the usual two and a
half hours, so Mike is very pleased with himself. Then on
the way down the corridor, he overhears some colleagues.
'He's like Ghengis Khan! You can't get a word in
edgeways, and he stamped all over us to rush things along.
I shan't be coming to meetings any more if he's in charge!'
Mike feels very embarrassed.

Meetings don't just have to achieve the business, they
also have to satisfy the members. Otherwise, they *feel* as if
things haven't been achieved. Mike did rather railroad
people to get things done, and clearly forgot that people
make meetings work.

SETTING AGENDAS

The **agenda** is a list of what is to be dealt with at a meeting.
It need not be a formal document – it simply needs to state:

- where and when the meeting will take place

- who is expected to attend

- a list of items to be discussed (**agenda items**).

It is usual that the first item on the agenda is approval of
the notes of the last meeting (called **minutes**), and the last
items are 'Any Other Business' and the date of the next
meeting. 'Any Other Business' allows discussion of items
that weren't on the agenda.

The most important thing about an agenda is that it goes
to people who are expected to attend early enough, so they

have time to prepare for the meeting if necessary. An agenda needs to be both realistic and purposeful.

Be realistic

Agendas need to be realistic. This means they need to be achievable within the time allowed – not too long.

Give purpose

Make agendas purposeful. This means letting people know the purpose of items, so they know what to expect. An item can be on an agenda for one of three reasons:

- to inform
- to consult
- to reach a decision.

Make sure members of meetings know *why* the item is on the agenda. For example, don't let people think they are going to discuss and decide on something, if the item is only there to inform them of what has already been agreed elsewhere.

Do your homework

- Has this item arisen before?
- If so, what happened then?
- Try to find out who supports and who opposes an item.
- Have an agreed fallback position – a compromise you can resort to if things are going badly.

Beware of timing

How do you allocate time to each item? Most people don't bother, which is why so many meetings take so long! If you allocate time, you have much more chance of achieving your business.

- Agree in advance a time limit for each item. This will

prevent meetings overrunning. You don't have to put a time limit on the agenda, you can set one in your own mind.

- Consider how important an item is. Allow more time for more important items.

- Consider the likely desire of people to speak on a subject. You may need to allow extra time for people to make their points on a contentious subject, even if it is a relatively minor item, to 'clear the air'.

- Don't confuse important items with urgent items. Remember importance and urgency (see Chapter 2)? Urgent items deserve a quick mention, but may not necessarily require much time.

Issue documentation
- Consider when to issue papers or documents in advance. Do you need opinions, reactions, decisions on the day? If so, would it help if people had relevant information in advance to read?

- Is there too much to take in during the day? If so, could some things be sent out in advance?

- *Can* the information be circulated in advance, or does it really need verbal explanation to avoid confusion?

CASE STUDY

Nikki produces the wrong figures
Nikki goes to the monthly sales meeting, and has prepared some figures because she saw 'Sales Receipts' on the agenda. When the item comes up, she is asked for figures, but not the ones she had thought were required. 'Sorry,' she says, confused, 'I've brought the latest figures – I didn't realise you wanted a prediction.' She feels bad enough, but it's even worse when she overhears someone muttering 'Didn't you even read the agenda?'

She had, but it wasn't clear. Although she didn't produce the agenda, when it was something that was open to interpretation, she should have checked.

GAINING PARTICIPATION

The five factors in achieving participation are:

- introductions
- motivation
- listening
- control
- summary.

The same principles apply, whether you are chairing or just attending a meeting – you can do all these things as an 'attendee' to help yourself and others participate effectively. However, let's assume you are 'in the chair' yourself.

Give introductions

- Introduce members on arrival. Introduce self as chairperson. Who feels strongly about which subjects? Does anyone have to leave early? If so, would it be helpful to rearrange the sequence of the agenda?

- Introduce new members. Introduce visitors, and arrange to deal with their agenda item as soon as possible.

- Introduce each item on the agenda concisely. Refer to past history where appropriate. Give clear indications of the purpose of the item on the agenda: to inform, consult or decide.

Give motivation

- Always remember that to encourage input, you may have to put someone on the spot.

- Be aware of specialist interests among those present.

- Bring in quiet members. Canvas opinions. Be open about needing input due to your own lack of detailed knowledge.

- Encourage contributions from members.

- To start debate, call on different viewpoints alternately. You must be seen to be balanced and give justice to all.

Listening

- Listening is an active behaviour – you need to be *seen* to be listening! Use nods, looks, eye contact, questions to clarify understanding.

- Always try to see and understand the other point of view.

- Listen to the minority.

Controlling

- Always remember that, above all else, people expect that the chairperson will do something to control the meeting.

- Control by choosing and using allies and enemies.

- Control by formality (formal procedures), timing (pacing the meeting and allocating timings) or behaviour.

- Control contributions, especially proposals, and keep track of debate direction. Steer discussions if necessary. Too light control means discussions wander; too heavy and you risk appearing to have your mind already made up.

- Control through courtesy.

- Do not let 'multiple meetings' start – they are distracting.

- Know when to give in, to preserve the integrity of your status as chairperson.

Summarising
- Give periodic summaries. Highlight key points and review progress.

- Give general summaries in technical discussions, to ensure understanding.

- Summarise at the meeting's end. This is a second chance to 'smooth any ruffled feathers', thank people for contributions, and remind members of agreed actions/tasks/responsibilities.

Holding pre-meetings
You can gain a preview of what may occur in a difficult, important meeting by having a pre-meeting, with only a few people rather than the full meeting.

Advantages
- They let you test opinions.

- You can iron out problems.

- You can 'strike deals'.

Disadvantages
- The meeting itself might appear a 'fait accompli'.

- You might get lulled into a false sense of security.

- You could alienate some people, by appearing to exclude them.

CASE STUDY

Bev's staff meeting runs out of time

Bev holds a staff meeting with all her shift members. She has a number of items to discuss, and writes out a list as a formal agenda. When the meeting starts, people want to discuss some things in more detail than Bev had anticipated, and she has difficulty controlling things. Towards the end, time gets short and so the last things on the list are discussed hardly at all, and Bev doesn't get the responses she needs on them.

Bev should have given the agenda to everyone so they could see how things were progressing. She should also have controlled things better, perhaps by introducing each topic and setting a time limit that was realistic. She could have pointed out what items were still to come before they actually ran out of time.

QUESTIONS AND ANSWERS

So are good meetings down to the chairperson then?
Usually. The best chairperson in the world won't stop some people, if they are determined to be difficult. But in most instances, a good chairperson can make a huge difference. In meetings where you are not chairing, don't rely on the chairperson – remember all the points on the previous pages, and put them into practice, and it will help enormously.

Do we have to have a chairperson?
No. This is too formal for some meetings. However, most meetings without a chairperson will find that someone 'takes over' and controls things – people have a natural tendency to expect someone to take charge. In many meetings, one person is more senior than the others, and people may naturally assume that those people will run the meeting.

What about motions and proposals and things?
If you ever attend any formal meetings where these are
used, you will need to look up exactly what procedures and
rules apply. However, for most people, these are
formalities they will never need to know about.

TAKING MINUTES

Notes of a meeting are called **minutes**. In a formal meeting,
a chairperson and secretary may be appointed. The
secretary's job is to send out the agenda and other papers,
and to take the minutes. In other meetings of a less formal
nature, a volunteer may take the minutes down on paper,
or the chairperson him/ herself may do this.

Who should take them?
It is not necessarily a good idea to take your own minutes
if you are in charge of a meeting. The advantage is that
you control what is written down. The disadvantage,
however, is that you have to control the meeting, listen,
understand and participate, and write notes all at once.
A better idea is to get someone else to do the minutes for
you.

How to format them
The format of minutes varies – some organisations have a
set format, in others you are free to produce them in your
own way. However they are laid out, minutes usually take
a certain sequence. A typical sequence is given below.

1. *Description*: A sentence saying what the meeting was,
   where and when it was held.

2. *Presence*: A list of people present, and a list of people
   unable to attend (called **apologies**).

3. *Minutes of the last meeting*: A statement saying whether
   everyone agreed that the minutes of the last meeting

were reasonably accurate, and detailing any discussions about them (called **matters arising**).

4. *Agenda items*: Notes on each item discussed in the same order as they appeared on the agenda. Details of any discussions made. Details of any action to be taken *must* be recorded. Include the name of who is to take action, so people know what they have to do.

5. *Any other business*: Anything discussed that was not on the agenda, recorded as for agenda items.

6. *Date of the next meeting*: The date of the next meeting is given.

Distributing minutes

It is usual to give everyone (including those who didn't attend) a copy of the minutes. Some people do this before the next meeting. Others prefer to send the minutes with the agenda for the next meeting, or even to give them out at the beginning of the next meeting.

MANAGEMENT TIPS

- Always keep your cool. Remember – control through courtesy.

- Be prepared for the worst, and even if it happens, you will be able to cope.

- Prepare in advance.

- Don't take things personally. Remember, you are discussing an item, not you and your management.

- Don't let discussions get personal.

- Don't be over-organised – be flexible enough to allow and encourage participation.

ACTION POINTS

1. Think of a meeting you have attended but not chaired. List the good things and bad things that either happened or that the chairperson did. How could things have been handled better?

2. When you next attend a meeting, keep a list of each member's name, and keep score of how many times they speak on each topic. Do some people dominate? Do some people fail to contribute? How could this be changed?

The material on pages 93 to 102 is reproduced with the kind permission of Mr Ritchie Stevenson.

7

Managing Your Team

UNDERSTANDING LEADERSHIP

What is the difference between management and leadership? The dictionary defines **management** as being in charge, controlling, administering, handling. **Leadership**, on the other hand, is defined as being the principal or 'front-runner', being an example, holding the chief role, as well as many of the list of definitions for management. Leadership is more *visible* somehow – the public face of management.

Of course, another consideration is that you cannot be a leader without followers. If you have no people, you can still be a manager (of resources, money, projects etc), but not a leader. A further distinction is that leaders tend to be elected, while managers tend to be appointed.

There are three components to any situation requiring a leader. These are:

- a leader
- a situation
- a group of people.

These three components have led to three theories on leadership. Just because there are three theories, it doesn't mean that only one is right and the other two must be wrong. All three have more than a grain of truth in them.

The leader – trait theory
It used to be thought that leaders were 'born not made' – that they were born with certain **traits** that made them a good leader. People believed leadership was a superiority

over others that people were born either with or without. Therefore, a born leader would emerge naturally in any group, because they would have the traits or qualities necessary to be a leader.

The problem with this is that when we look at great leaders in history, the traits they possessed are not all the same. Consider Adolf Hitler and Mahatma Gandhi – both great leaders of their time, but with vastly differing qualities or traits. Physical differences occur too – consider General de Gaulle and Napoleon Bonaparte – one tall, the other short, and both great French leaders.

Improving your trait leadership

Develop your abilities as much as you can. Yes, some abilities you are either born with or not, such as a magnetic personality, but there are many other abilities you can work on:

- ability to see opportunities

- adaptability

- analysis

- communication

- decision-making

- dependability

- enthusiasm

- imagination

- integrity

- open-mindedness

- positive thinking

- reliability

- sincerity

- single-mindedness

- understanding

- willingness

and many, many more.

The situation – situational theory
This theory says that there is no such thing as a born leader, but that there are a whole variety of characteristics that might make a person a good leader, which people have a mixture of. In any situation, the person best suited to that **situation** will emerge as leader.

We can all imagine this – in a crisis, we usually look to someone who knows what to do, or who seems to be in control. In a different situation, exactly the same group of people might look to a completely different person for leadership.

This theory says that leaders rise to *power* – to have authority. There are three main sources of power that a leader can build on: position, personality and expertise.

Position
This is status, position or rank. Some people are seen as powerful because they have status, or are appointed to a certain position or rank. Examples would be Alexander the Great, Queen Victoria or General Custer.

Personality
This is character, or charisma. Some people are seen as powerful because they have a powerful character or personality. Examples would be Lawrence of Arabia, Napoleon Bonaparte, Mahatma Gandhi, John F. Kennedy.

Expertise
This is knowledge, experience or skill. Some people are seen to be powerful because of their knowledge or skill or experience. A good historical example would be Isambard Kingdom Brunel.

Improving your situational leadership

Develop power or authority relevant to situations you commonly find yourself in. If you have low status, develop knowledge and experience to compensate. Try to stay adaptable, so you have something relevant to contribute in all work situations.

- Plan.

- Take advantage of any available training.

- Keep updated about things around you.

- Find out about areas you are weak in.

- Talk to people – try to learn from others.

- Keep in close contact with your boss – keep them up-to-date.

- Learn to work with staff representatives and trade union representatives.

- Get to know other managers and build relationships with them.

- Think ahead, anticipate likely events, then prepare for them.

The group – functional theory

The third theory on leadership, John Adair's theory, says that any group has a number of functions it needs to perform – a number of needs that need to be fulfilled. The leader will be the one who can best satisfy those needs. These needs are in three categories: team, task and individual needs.

- *Team*: The group of people needs to be drawn together and organised so they co-operate with each other.

- *Task*: The task the group is faced with needs to be achieved.

- *Individual*: Individuals need to be recognised and

utilised appropriately – they need to use their skills and talents when they can.

A good leader must concentrate on all three functions or needs. Too much attention to the team may mean that individuals become dissatisfied, or the task is not achieved. Too much attention to the task, and the team and individuals may work poorly together, then friction and dissatisfaction may result. Too much attention to individuals, and the team may pull apart, and the task not be achieved.

Improving your functional leadership
Be aware of the three functions, and do not neglect any of them. Acquire knowledge and expertise in dealing with tasks, teams and individuals.

Task
- Set standards, and maintain them.

- Monitor and evaluate performance.

- Set realistic and achievable objectives, both for yourself and for others.

Team
- Let people know that personal gain is not as important as team achievement.

- Communicate regularly.

- Encourage co-operation and compromise in the event of differences among team members.

- Keep everyone informed of progress.

Individual
- Explain what is to be done, why and how.

- Encourage people to be more involved.

- Get to know people.

- Help people develop their skills.

- Delegate wherever possible.

- Recognise people's achievements and contributions.

- Make any criticism constructive.

CASE STUDY

Bev worries about leadership

Bev is in charge of her people, but worries that she isn't a good leader. She feels leadership is being inspiring and looked up to. One day, she approaches Matron for advice, as she is thinking of some team leadership training. Matron laughs. 'The only person who doesn't think you're a good leader is you!' she jokes.

Bev needs to remember that good leadership often revolves around tasks, teamwork, and individuals. By looking after each of these, she is doing a good job, without being charismatic or stylish. She is doing exactly the right thing by seeking some extra training, to boost her skills and confidence.

MOTIVATING OTHERS

You can't be a leader without followers – you need other people. So now we are going to look at how to motivate people.

Motivation is what makes people act in a particular way – what 'makes them tick'. Understanding this is important for a manager, because if you know *why* people do things, it makes it easier to persuade them to do the things you want them to do. It makes it easier to get things done.

One of the main tasks of management is to influence other people to do something – often things they would not normally want to do. Understanding people's **motives** – their reasons for doing or not doing a thing – can help us do this.

Basically, people have **needs**. A need is a lack of something – something we want. This produces a **drive**, or a motive in us to satisfy that need. This motivates us. Satisfying this need, or getting the thing we want or lack, is our **goal**.

Needs

Maslow's theory of motivation is called the 'hierarchy of needs'. Maslow thought that people have five main needs in the following order of importance:

- *Physiological needs*   – the need to eat
  – the need to drink
  – the need to work
  – the need to sleep
  – the need to reproduce

- *Safety needs*   – the need for shelter
  – the need to feel secure

- *'Belonging' needs*   – the need to feel part of a group
  – the need for acceptance

- *Self-esteem needs*   – the need to feel good about themselves
  – the need to be recognised for achievement

- *Self-realisation needs* – the need for personal fulfilment
  – the need to grow and develop

Maslow believed that people would not move on down this list to be motivated by the next set of needs until the previous set(s) had been satisfied.

Another theory – by Alderfer – categorised these needs into only three groups:

- existence needs

- relatedness needs

- growth needs.

This simplifies the issue – we have needs to maintain us physically, needs to relate to others, and needs to develop and grow as individuals.

Remember, everyone is different – some people come to work to earn money (existence needs) and have no desire either to 'get on' with others (relatedness needs), or earn promotion (growth needs). Others work to meet people and have a personal challenge and sense of achievement (relatedness needs). Others work to gain experience to move their career forward (growth needs). Obviously, many people work for a combination of reasons.

Motivating people by filling existence needs
- Pay people appropriately for the work they do.

- Make sure the workplace is safe, and a good environment to work in.

- Give people enough work to do.

- Give people incentives – prizes or bonuses. Beware – this can be dangerous, as some people will not respond, and some will be demotivated because they think they have no chance of 'winning'.

- Recognise people's need for privacy – give them their 'own space'.

- Try to arrange work so people see the end result.

- Set goals so people know what they are doing.

- Treat people as individuals.

Motivating people by filling relatedness needs
- Show respect for people – listen to them and express an interest in them.

- Give people responsibility – delegate.

- Give recognition – thank people, and acknowledge achievement and effort.

- Communicate openly with people.

- Involve people in decision-making.

- Encourage ideas and suggestions.

- Praise people for effort as well as achievement – a thing doesn't have to be perfect to be praised.

- Get to know people and make sure they know others.

- Keep in contact – exchange information regularly.

Motivating people by filling growth needs
- Offer support and help to do new tasks.

- Give people a challenge where possible.

- Make work interesting.

- Encourage people to think for themselves.

- Keep people informed about new information and developments appropriate to them.

- Ask people what motivates them, and give them the chance to do it whenever possible.

- Give people new work, when possible, to 'stretch' them.

- Offer training when possible. This does not have to be a course – you can do things like advise them on reading, or set up sessions where people work with others to learn more about others' work.

CASE STUDY

Nikki decides to try to motivate her staff
Nikki buys some books for the office, and takes photocopies of any relevant magazines articles to pass round. This way, she feels people are keeping up-to-date,

112

so she gives them demanding work where she can, to give them a challenge and more responsibility. She even sets up a 'shadowing' programme, where they spend one day a week with another member of staff, learning about their job. Jacquie doesn't respond, and if anything seems less motivated than before. When Nikki asks what's wrong, Jacquie says, 'I don't feel part of all this Nikki. I don't want to take on more – I took this job because I liked it, and I liked the people I'd be working with. Now nobody has time to talk much any more.'

Nikki should remember that there is little point focusing on higher needs for motivation unless the lower needs have been satisfied. Jacquie is cleary motivated by social needs, and just wants to do her job well and work with people she likes. She isn't motivated by advancement or development at the moment, so offering these won't motivate her.

QUESTIONS AND ANSWERS

How can you tell if people are motivated or not?
If people are not motivated (demotivated), you may see some of the following:

- increased sickness

- increased absenteeism

- lateness

- poor quality work

- lack of communication

- attitude

- emotional levels rise – frustration, short-temperedness etc.

So why do people become demotivated?
- lack of recognition

- boredom/lack of interest or stimulation

- lack of involvement

- not being listened to

- lack of encouragement

- lack of training

- poor or no delegation

- criticism

- too much or too little work.

If I had to pick one thing that motivates people, which is the most important?
Recognition. Most other factors involve recognition in some way. Demotivated people may be late, for example, or absent, or get angry and short-tempered in order to be noticed. This is nothing more than a disguised search for recognition, which the individuals may not even be aware of. So, recognition produces motivation, while lack of recognition demotivates people.

WORKING AS A TEAM

Why work as a team?

Creativity
- Teams are usually more creative than individuals.

- Teams tend to produce more ideas.

Satisfaction
- Teamworking can provide good opportunities for personal development and learning.

- Individuals find increased motivation from working in a team.

- Responsibility is shared, so individuals feel more committed to the work.

- Energy and excitement tends to be greater.

- A sense of belonging and pride can be generated.

- A team contains a larger range of experience and abilities than any one individual.

Skills
- Skills and abilities can be utilised fully.

- Some tasks simply cannot be done by an individual.

Speed/productivity
- Things can be done faster – 'many hands make light work'.

- Productivity is usually higher, as teamwork focuses effort and skills.

- A wider range of work can be undertaken.

Evaluation
- Teams evaluate ideas from more viewpoints than an individual could, so ideas tend to be better evaluated.

- Analysis and judgement can be more objective in a team, although teams can take more risks, as individuals feel less personally responsible.

Obviously, there are many tasks which it would not be appropriate to carry out as a team. Simple or routine tasks are best dealt with by individuals, and also decisions which can be logically calculated or deduced.

Selecting a team size
The size of team you should use varies – there are advantages and disadvantages of having large or small teams. Consider the following points when deciding how many to include in your team:

- *Vulnerability*: The smaller the team, the more vulnerable it is – replacing just one team member can upset the whole team, and one member being absent can be critical. In a large team, substitutions and absences can be handled more easily.

- *Relationships*: The smaller the team, the closer the relationships between team members.

- *Individuality*: The larger the team, the less individuality members have. A large team can take on 'mob mentality', where people stop thinking of themselves, and simply go along with the team, regardless of whether they would normally agree or not. The larger the group, the greater the pressure for conformity.

- *Control*: The larger the team, the harder it is to control – the more organisation and direction it needs. With large teams, a structure may need to be developed, with sub-groups.

SETTING OBJECTIVES

The best way to make sure people stay focused on a task is to set objectives, for individuals as well as for teams. Objectives are performance goals or targets. They are specific results or situations that a person or group is expected to achieve within a given time-frame.

Setting objectives is important for several reasons:

- They show individuals and teams what direction to work towards.

- They give a means of measuring achievement.

- They motivate – people are motivated by achievement and recognition.

- They prevent wasted effort.

How to set objectives

1. Agree objectives jointly. Remember, people are more committed to a thing, and more likely to take responsibility, if they have been involved in it.

2. Agree the measures of achievement. If an objective cannot be measured, you will not be able to assess whether it has been achieved or not.

3. Be specific if possible. The more specific you are, the easier it will be to see whether the objective has been achieved satisfactorily.

4. Agree a realistic time scale. If you don't set a time limit, it may never get done.

5. Make the objectives achievable but challenging. Setting unrealistic objectives is demotivating.

6. Let the person who is to achieve the objective decide how to do it.

7. Use objectives for personal development – to stretch and teach people.

8. Review progress regularly.

CASE STUDY

Mike loses his leadership

Mike sets individual objectives monthly, and he allocates all the work to people as it comes in. Large tasks he tends to split into small sections, and give these to individuals. He has always tried to set work appropriate to people's skills and experience. One day, he notices that Rachel is doing work he had given to Tom. On further investigation, he discovers that this is happening all the time – people are re-allocating work behind his back so they can all do the tasks they like best.

Mike has lost control, as he has focused on the task and fragmenting it into subtasks. He has lost sight of the overall team and the advantages of working as one. Setting objectives is good, but he needs to be more specific so people know not to re-allocate work.

MANAGEMENT TIPS

- Try and improve your leadership skills.

- Be aware of tasks, teams and individuals, and give them all an appropriate amount of attention.

- Be aware of people's needs and motives – including your own.

- Motivate people appropriately – remember not everyone is motivated by the same things.

- Tackle demotivation – if you leave it, it may spread to others.

- Give recognition wherever possible.

- Work as a team.

- Set objectives – for yourself, for others and for teams.

- Monitor performance by whether objectives are being met, and give recognition where possible.

ACTION POINTS

1. Go through the list of traits that a leader can develop. Write objectives to help you develop those you need to improve on. For example: *Open-mindedness* – develop my open-mindedness by encouraging others to make suggestions to me and considering each fully. Aim to double the amount of suggestions I receive each week within six months.

2. Do you ever feel demotivated? Why? What can you do to prevent this in others?

3. Examine any teams you are a part of. Do they work well, or not? Why?

8

Managing Staff

Figure 13 shows the sequence of defining and filling a job. Time could be saved by omitting one or more steps, but only by doing each step will you be sure of appointing the best person for the job. You also need to ensure you have been fair and complied with relevant employment legislation and not been discriminatory in any way.

DEFINING WHO AND WHAT YOU WANT

Considering options
When a vacancy arises, you don't necessarily just have to recruit a replacement: other options might be better. Consider the following:

Part-time/full-time
Could several part-time staff do the job of one full-time staff? This can give more flexibility.

Temporary/permanent/fixed term contract
Is a permanent replacement necessary? If the future is uncertain, temporary staff or a fixed term contract (a contract until a certain date) might be beneficial.

Secondment
Could someone in another department or section gain experience from doing the job for a while (a **secondment**)?

Redistribution of duties
Could the work be done by redistributing it amongst existing staff? If it could, this could save money.

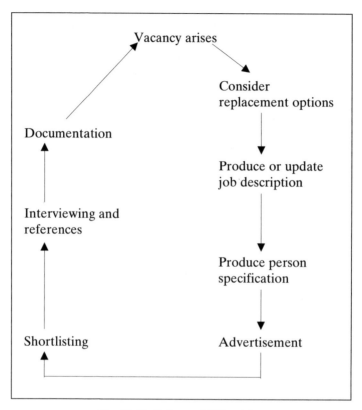

Fig. 13. Defining and filling jobs.

Describing jobs and people

After reviewing the options, the next stage is to produce a
job description and **person specification**. These are written
descriptions of the job and the person you want to do it,
that you use to help you choose the right person for the
job. The person specification is especially important in
helping you avoid discrimination.

Job descriptions

If you are simply replacing someone, you may already have
a job description. If so, it must be checked so it is

up-to-date and accurately reflects what you actually want the new person to do.

If you don't already have a job description, for example if it is a new job, it is good practice to produce one. Many organisations have a standard format for this, but the main points to be included are set out below.

Remember, when the successful person accepts the job, you should get them to sign a copy of the job description, to show they accept these duties as the job, and they agree to carry out all the duties listed.

The job
- Job title.

- Department and section.

Purpose
- The purpose of the job.

- Objectives of the job (quantified where possible).

- Duties involved and methods of carrying them out.

Responsibilities
- Any responsibility for developing or recommending changes.

- Responsibilities for equipment, people, money etc.

Relationships
- Who the job liaises with.

- To whom the job is accountable.

- Other relationships that influence achievement of objectives.

Physical conditions
- Where the job is.

- Hours of work.

- Accident or health risks.

Pay and conditions
- Salary range.

- Bonus or incentive schemes if any.

- Pensions.

- Sickness entitlement.

- Holiday entitlement.

- Car or other allowances.

Any other duties
- It is good practice to include an 'any other duties' clause, stating that the post-holder is required to carry out any other duties within reason. This enables you to give them duties that are not in their job description when necessary – it gives you flexibility.

Describing people

The **person specification** is the job description translated into human terms. Without this, you cannot define the type of person you are looking for.

You simply list the essential requirements, or **criteria**. Human nature means that we often tend to come up with a specification for superman or superwoman, and no one could ever match this, so try to keep criteria realistic. Criteria should only be set if the job could not be performed to the required standard without them.

The person specification need not be a formal document, but ensure the following do not get overlooked:

Physical factors
- What are the requirements in terms of physical ability and health?

- Consider height, build, hearing, eyesight, general health.

- Requirements in terms of appearance.

- Consider looks, grooming, dress, voice.
- Beware of prejudice.

Skills and knowledge
- What knowledge and skills are needed to do the job?
- What qualifications are needed?
- What experience or past training is needed?
- How much experience in other jobs is required?

Emotional factors
- How important is it that the person be able to get on with others?
- What ability for leadership is needed?
- Is stability (steadiness and dependability) important?
- Is self-reliance – independent thought and working – necessary?

Personal circumstances
- Is mobility needed?
- Is nearness of home to the job relevant?
- Do they need to be able to work irregular hours?
- What personal circumstances would prevent someone from doing the job?
- Again, be especially aware of prejudice and discrimination in this area.

Make a list of all the factors on a sheet of paper. Mark each item as **essential** or **desirable**. Essential shows a person could not do the job without it. Desirable simply means you would prefer the person to fit your list in this respect, but they could still do the job if they didn't.

Now you have a good profile of who you want – what

sort of person. By comparing people with your list, you can be sure you will choose the right person, *objectively*, without prejudice or discrimination.

CASE STUDY

Bev replaces Sarah the cook with June

Bev doesn't bother drawing up a person specification for a new cook to replace Sarah, thinking she has a pretty good idea of what she's looking for. At the interviews, June stands out as a good applicant, perhaps because she is quite similar to Sarah in a lot of ways. After a few weeks, however, it becomes apparent that June is a disaster. She is always taking time off (unlike Sarah), and her cooking is very limited in range.

Bev should have been objective, and listed what she did want from the new person. That way, she would have recruited someone more suitable, not someone she liked.

ADVERTISING

There are many ways of advertising vacancies. The most usual are:

- adverts in a newspaper or magazine, even the Internet
- cards in Jobcentres
- cards in shop windows
- noticeboards
- recruitment or advertising agencies (note that these normally charge you a fee for finding you the right person)
- staff newsletters.

Do not forget to advertise internally. Someone working in another part of your organisation might want to apply, or a member of staff may know someone looking for a similar job. Internal advertising is usually free.

Remember that advertising in newspapers and magazines can be expensive. Unless you are in a rush, you could always try cheaper methods first (such as noticeboards, shop windows or Jobcentres), to see whether you get a good response, before moving on to expensive advertising in papers and magazines.

Content of advertisements

Whatever method you decide on, be as specific and detailed as possible in your advertisement. This will give you as suitable a group of applicants as possible. It is a waste of time and money dealing with unsuitable applicants. Be sure to include:

- where the job is
- the salary or pay
- the hours
- any essential criteria such as a requirement for shorthand or particular qualifications
- a date by which to apply
- how you would like them to apply
  - by letter
  - by sending a curriculum vitae (CV)
  - by telephone
  - in person
  - on an application form.

SHORTLISTING APPLICANTS

Step one – compare with the person specification

Once you have all the applications, go through each one against the person specification. Use a copy of your list of factors, and eliminate any applications that do not fit all

particular group, because less people in that group would be able to meet the criteria

- using tests which are not necessary for success at the job – this may discriminate against people whose first language is not English

- requiring some groups to undertake tests which other groups do not have to perform

- asking questions of one group which you do not ask of another group.

If someone feels that have been unfairly discriminated against, they can take you to an industrial tribunal.

INTERVIEWING

Interviews have two **aims**:

- To confirm and expand on the information you already have about the applicant.

- To give the applicant more information about the job.

Interviews may sound simple, but they are **difficult** for two reasons:

- The interviewer only has a limited amount of time to find out all they need.

- Interviews are stressful. This may cause both interviewer and interviewee to behave unnaturally.

To overcome this, the interviewer needs to remember several **key points**:

- Control the interview by questioning.

- Establish rapport to reduce the stress, so the interviewee can be as natural as possible.

- Listen and observe. Be sensitive to all information.

- Prepare thoroughly, so interview time is used to best advantage.

- Structure the content of the interview so they get the information they want.

QUESTIONS AND ANSWERS

I worry about what sorts of questions to ask at interviews. What sort are best?
Questions should be aimed at assessing people's suitability against the essential or desirable criteria you have set. They should be mainly about work experience, qualifications, skills, abilities and aptitudes. They should relate to the requirements of the job. If personal circumstances may affect performance in the job (e.g. if working unsocial hours is required), this should be discussed objectively without detailed questions about family circumstances. Questions which may imply discrimination must be avoided.

Can I really ask questions about all my criteria? Some of them are difficult to ask about without being personal, or possibly discriminating?
Genuine criteria which it may prove the most difficult to probe (because valid questions may be misinterpreted) are those relating to availability during all likely working hours, commitment to a regular permanent job, or career aspirations. If you have to probe these matters, put questions in such a way that they apply equally to all interviewees. Then, actually ask them of all interviewees, not just some. Examples would be:

1. Have you any commitments that might mean you need time off other than for holidays?

2. How long do you intend remaining in this job?

How can I be sure I have not discriminated unfairly?
Remember, it is not sufficient for an interviewer to *think*
they have not discriminated unfairly, or to *believe* they
have used fair criteria. It must be possible to *show*, if
challenged, that rational criteria were applied, and that
applicants have no valid reason for feeling discrimination
has happened. Thus, you need to know the job
requirements, to judge against them and only them, and to
keep records for at least six months after an appointment is
made. Records should include references, and notes made
at interview. Therefore, interviewers should note briefly in
writing why the successful applicant was chosen, and if
possible, why the others were not.

INDUCTING NEW EMPLOYEES

When new staff start work, they need to know many things
before they are truly settled in and their work is
productive. To ensure that they are able to contribute to
the organisation as quickly as possible, set time aside to
induct them – to make them part of the organisation.

Research shows that new people are most likely to leave
within their first few weeks, so concentrate on making
them feel part of the team at the earliest opportunity. Your
organisation may have an **induction course** for new
employees. If so, do not assume it covers everything – still
check if there is anything you need to cover yourself.

As a rough guide, try to cover all of the following with
new employees. This should give them a good induction to
work.

Documentation and procedures
- Completion of time sheets or clocking arrangements.
- Payday and method of payment.
- Bonus, productivity or incentive schemes.
- What to do in the event of sickness or absence.

- How to book holidays.

Introductions
- Introductions to colleagues.

- Introduction to their job – main duties.

- Introduction to contacts outside immediate workplace, if any.

- Introduction to supervisor and/or manager.

Working arrangements
- Workplace.

- Hours of work.

- Tea and coffee breaks.

- Canteen, cloakroom, staff room and toilet facilities etc.

- Issue of any equipment, tools etc.

- Relation of their job to others' work.

Emergency and safety
- Emergency procedures.

- Fire precautions and drills.

- First aid location.

- Safety policy, procedures and practices.

General information
- Description of department, section, organisation.

- Structure of department or section and names of key personnel.

- Trade union membership – where to join.

- Holidays – entitlement, timing etc.

- Pension/superannuation – rate of deductions etc.

- Grievance procedures – how to make a grievance.

- Disciplinary procedures, and workplace rules etc.

- Available training schemes.

- Personnel policies.

The best thing of all is to make **time** for the new person. Try to set aside some time every day for at least the first week or so, to talk to them and see how they are doing.

CASE STUDY

Nikki's trainee annoys a senior manager
Nikki has a college trainee, Frances, to work in the office on a placement scheme for three months. As she will only be there for a short time, Nikki doesn't bother sending her on the company Induction course, but instead inducts her herself in things like fire exits, health and safety etc. A few weeks after the placement is over, a senior manager calls Nikki in to speak to him. 'Look at this!' he exclaims, waving a college report, 'Frances obviously has no idea how we're organised, and she's gone back and written up a college project on the company. She draws the conclusion we're structured wrongly, and work is duplicated, wasting time and money. The Managing Director is furious!'

Both Nikki and the manager know Frances has drawn the wrong conclusion. She didn't know there are some very good reasons for the structure, which produce massive savings and synergies elsewhere. However, as she hadn't been inducted, she had no idea about the structure or why it is that way. Nikki should send everyone on induction, even if they will only be there for a relatively short while.

TRAINING PEOPLE

Why train people?
- To enable the job to be done properly.

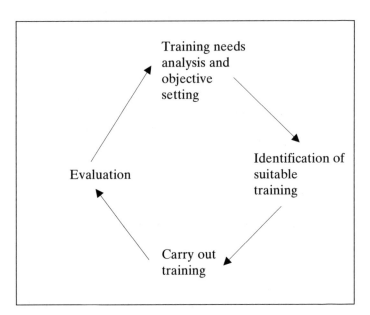

Fig. 14. The training cycle.

- To maintain quality.
- To maintain quantity.
- To meet legal requirements.
- To give management flexibility.
- To develop a member of staff.
- To give someone a boost – increase morale and motivation.
- To prepare someone for a forthcoming change in job/work.

People don't need to go away on a training course – there are many ways of training people, including working alongside an experienced employee (on the job training), following manuals and instruction books, project work, secondments and team-working.

Fig. 14 shows the training cycle, the various stages of which are explained in the following paragraphs.

Training needs analysis
A **training need** is a shortfall in performance that training could correct. Talk to people and see what they feel they lack in terms of skills, knowledge and understanding. Then look at their performance and experience, and see what you feel they lack in terms of skills, knowledge and experience. Fig. 15 shows the equation.

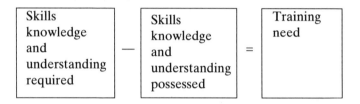

Fig. 15. Training needs analysis equation.

Many organisations use appraisals as an opportunity to discuss training needs. However, training needs don't always occur just before appraisals, so be watchful for them at any time.

Set objectives for the training need, so you and the person to be trained both know what you will get out of it. For example:

Training need: Needs to be able to use new word processor.

Objective: To be able to use new word processor unsupervised, but with occasional reference to the manual, after attending two-day training course.

Identification of suitable training
Find out how to train the person to fill the training need.

- Can you teach them yourself?

- Can they read what they need to know from manuals or books?

- Is there a training course?

- Could they work with someone experienced and learn from them?

Carry out the training
Give the person a date and time when they will be trained and stick to it. Make sure the person carrying out the training knows what objective(s) you have set for the trainee.

Evaluation
After training has taken place, evaluate. This means check whether the training has worked or not – don't assume that just because someone has been trained the objective has now been met and everything will be all right. Go back to the objective(s) you set and ask whether they have been met. If not, you may have to take a look at further training or extra support.

CASE STUDY

Mike's training isn't effective
A new computer system is installed, so Mike arranges some training. Afterwards, only Rachel seems to have completely got the hang of it, so people go to her for help and advice. Eventually, there is a problem with the system, and errors come to light.

Mike should have evaluated the training, to make sure it was effective. Even if he didn't, he should certainly have arranged some follow-up training when it became obvious that people weren't confident and capable using the new system. He should know you can't just send people on a course and expect them to learn.

MANAGEMENT TIPS

- Define exactly who and what you want before starting to look for it.

- Don't automatically replace someone with a similar person. Consider all your options for getting that work done.

- Make advertisements specific, so you attract a set of applicants that are very close to what you are looking for. This will save you time.

- Use the criteria to shortlist, and keep records.

- Be objective, and try to avoid discriminating.

- Induct new employees properly.

- When training needs are detected, act to fill them with appropriate training.

ACTION POINTS

1. Choose a member of staff at work. If they left tomorrow, how many different ways could you arrange for their workload to be carried out?

2. With the same member of staff in mind, assume you are replacing them. Draw up a new job description, or go through their current one and see whether this is what you really want. Draw up a person specification.

3. Going back to point 2, compare the job description and person specification with the member of staff you currently have. How do they differ? Draw up a training needs analysis for the person to address any differences between their current skills, knowledge and experience and those you want.

9

Managing People Problems

APPRAISING STAFF

Appraisals are reviews of an employee's performance.
They are generally in the form of a one-to-one interview
with their manager or supervisor at regular intervals, from
which a written record is made. Your organisation may
have its own appraisal or performance review system, but
you can also do your own, even if no formal system exists.

Why do appraisals?
- To objectively examine an individual's performance
  over a given period of time.

- To get feedback from an individual on how they think
  they are doing, and their hopes for the future.

- To agree future performance targets.

What are the advantages of appraisals?

For the employee
- They learn how they are getting on (their performance).

- It ensures their efforts are acknowledged and
  appreciated.

- It identifies improvements that need to be made in
  performance.

- It maps out future career prospects.

For the manager
- Better understanding of employees.

- Better co-operation from staff.

- It reviews performance of staff.

- They gain an insight into the employee's ideas about the job.

- It helps identify future potential.

For the organisation
- It makes staff more committed.

- Personal relationships improve.

- Effectiveness and efficiency improve.

- It helps to plan future allocation of work.

How to carry out an appraisal interview

1. Review the person's file and history in advance. Look at their job description.

2. Make arrangements for the interview in advance:

- Book a room where you will not be disturbed.

- Give the person notice of the appraisal.

- Reassure them – many people find appraisals nerve-wracking.

3. Carry out the interview as informally as possible. Let them participate. Discuss:

- *Past*   – how they think they've done
            – how they have done

- *Present*   – how they think they're doing
            – how they are doing

- *Future*   – what they would like to do or think they
              might do
            – what you think they should do or could do.

4. Agree a plan of action. Set objectives.

5. Write a record of the interview (and ideally, get the person to sign it).

6. Monitor and help them throughout the next period, so they can achieve the action plan and objectives set for them.

Why do appraisals go wrong?

- Failure to prepare enough.

- Failure to prepare at all.

- Failure to face up to or tackle problem areas.

- Failure to tackle problems constructively (getting personal).

- Failure to agree on a realistic course of action.

- Failure to take the appraisal seriously.

CASE STUDY

Nikki starts doing staff appraisals

Appraisals are a new to some people, and during them it is obvious to Nikki that people are focused on how they have done – the past. They are reluctant to discuss the future and their prospects. Nikki becomes quite frustrated.

Nikki should remember that many people find appraisals frightening, and worry they are going to be told they haven't done a good job. She should speak to people before carrying them out, to reassure them and make it clear what is expected.

HANDLING GRIEVANCES

A **grievance** is a formal or official complaint made by an employee. Even if not made in writing, take these seriously. Some organisations have a grievance procedure for you to follow. In any event, a good rule would be to always follow these steps.

1. *Listen*: listen fully to the complaint and acknowledge it.

2. *Investigate*: see whether the complaint is founded or not. Be objective.

3. *Take action*: address the source of the complaint if possible. If the complaint turns out to be unfounded, take action to prove this to the employee.

4. *Feedback*: always tell the person who made the complaint or grievance what you are going to do about it and why. Do this even if you are going to do nothing. Preferably, feedback to them in writing – give them a written copy of what you tell them.

QUESTIONS AND ANSWERS

What happens if someone complains during an appraisal?
Grievances should not be dealt with at appraisals. Appraisals are for discussing the employee who is having the appraisal, not others or their manager. Similarly, disciplinary matters should not be discussed at appraisal, but should be handled separately. By keeping discipline and grievance separate from appraisal, appraisals will be more constructive. If the complaint is about something specific that you can quickly and easily deal with, fine. But if it is 'messy', or a complaint about someone rather than something, keep it separate.

If an employee keeps complaining after I have answered their complaint, do I have to keep taking it seriously?
If there are a lot of minor complaints, it depends on what they are about. Don't confuse a grumble with an official complaint. An employee wishing to make an official

141

complaint, or grievance, should be asked to put it in writing so a record can be kept, and if they take it seriously themselves, they will. Minor grumbles are part of life, and should be dealt with on a less formal basis. How do you tell whether the complaint is serious or not? Well, if they are prepared to put it in writing, they usually view it as serious.

Do I have to have a proper interview for an appraisal? I don't really have the time.
No, of course not. There is nothing wrong with just having a quick chat now and again, but most people appreciate you taking the time to have a short interview with them, in private, to discuss their performance and prospects. Otherwise, a regular short chat is sufficient, provided you allow for privacy if someone needs it to discuss something.

DEALING WITH PERFORMANCE PROBLEMS

Sometimes a performance problem can be dealt with at appraisal. More often, it needs dealing with separately – it would be ridiculous to 'save up' problems for the appraisal once every year or six months! If people aren't performing satisfactorily, talk to them.

Identifying the gap
Specify exactly what the gap is between their performance and the required performance. Ideally, get them to agree that there is a gap – then they are far more likely to do something about it. Ways of proving that a gap exists include:

- customer complaints

- others doing similar work for comparison

- record cards

- rejected work

142

- sickness and absence records
- testimony of people who come into contact with them
- time sheets
- training needs analysis
- unfinished work.

Establishing reasons for the gap

There are many reasons for poor performance. Some of them are listed below:

- domestic circumstances
- emotional problems
- family problems
- job has changed
- lack of intellectual ability
- lack of motivation
- lack of physical ability
- lack of training
- lack of understanding
- personality clash with boss
- personality clash with others
- poor discipline
- poor health
- poor management
- poor pay
- too little confidence
- too much confidence
- unreliable equipment.

Try to establish which reason(s) apply, and whether they are in your control, or not. They may be outside the individual's control, so the gap cannot be closed at present; for example, in the case of poor health.

Closing the gap
Set objectives for closing the gap – in stages if necessary. Review these regularly, reviewing progress.

What to do about unresolved problems
If a problem is not resolved after a reasonable period of time, you should consider taking disciplinary action.

CASE STUDY

Mike is seen as unfair
Mike establishes a gap in Tom's performance. He sets objectives, and waits to see an improvement. After a period of time, there is no noticeable change in Tom's work, and he hears that other staff are 'behind Tom', and think Mike has been unfair. Tom has obviously been discussing the situation with others.

Of course, Mike can't stop Tom discussing matters. But if he had got Tom to accept the gap, things might have been different. If people don't accept there is a gap, natural reactions are to feel victimised and frustrated. Mike needs to spend time with Tom and show clear evidence that the gap exists.

DISPENSING DISCIPLINE

Disciplinary procedures
Most organisations have a disciplinary procedure, which you need to follow whenever you have a disciplinary problem. Most procedures follow stages. A common sequence is this:

1. *Informal warning/discussion*: an informal, 'off-the-record' talk about the problem.

2. *Verbal warning*: this is usually the first stage of **formal** procedures. A verbal warning is given, and a note saying that this has been done is placed on the employee's record or file.

3. *Written warning*: the employee is given a warning in writing, detailing the problem. A copy is placed on the employee's record or file.

4. *Final warning*: this is the same as a written warning, but the employee is warned that any further occurrence of the problem will lead to dismissal.

5. *Dismissal*: this is usually a last resort. The employee is dismissed. This usually follows a final warning, but sometimes for a very serious breach of discipline, an employee could be suspended or dismissed immediately, without going through the other stages. This is referred to as **instant dismissal**.

Preventing disciplinary problems

- Be approachable – that way you find out about problems before they occur or become serious.

- Be consistent and fair.

- Ensure people know all the rules and standards:
  – at induction
  – at regular intervals.

- Establish good relationships – get to know people.

- Feed back regularly – let people know how they are doing.

- Foster teamwork.

- Remember the importance of recognition – praise people when they do well.

- Set a good example.

- Set targets and make sure people are aware of them.

- Train people adequately to do the job.

Dealing with disciplinary problems

Procedures
- Know your organisation's procedures.

- Know your part in those procedures.

- Know the limits of your authority – when do you need to call for more senior management to get involved?

Timing
- Deal with things as soon as possible – 'nip things in the bud' before they get worse.

- Deal with things in private – never discipline in front of others if you can possibly avoid it.

- Don't put things off because they are unpleasant.

- Don't rush things – you have to give the person the opportunity to speak and explain.

- Put a time limit on their improvement – set a date.

Practicalities
- Stay calm and objective. If you find yourself becoming angry, call a break and set a time to speak to them again, when you have calmed down.

- Be prepared. Have all the information and facts at hand. They may deny there is a problem, and so be prepared to prove it to them.

- Don't become subjective – you are dealing with a practical problem, not personalities. Stay focused on what the problem is.

- Get them to talk to you.

- Keep written records of what was said and done. Tell the person what will go on their record or personal file, so they know where they stand.

Monitoring and review
- Don't 'breathe down people's necks' after a disciplinary action. It is very demotivating. You do need to keep an eye on them, but don't make them think they are being watched.

- Praise them when they improve.

- If they do not improve within the agreed time scale, be ready to progress to the next stage of the disciplinary process.

CASE STUDY

Bev fails to use correct disciplinary procedures
Bev repeatedly has to warn Karen about her lack of performance. Just about everything she does is below standard. After a while, Bev discussed the situation with Matron, and they agree they should dismiss Karen. Unfortunately, all Bev's warnings have all been informal. As there is no record of them, so all they can do is give her yet another warning, and wait until next time to issue a written one.

Bev needs to check the disciplinary process and use it. If she had taken appropriate action from the start, things would be better now, and they would be able to take the necessary action.

COUNSELLING PEOPLE

Counselling is:

- analysing a problem

- assisting with stimulating someone's thoughts

- giving someone your undivided attention

- identifying with someone

- listening

- providing support.

Counselling is *not* about:

- giving advice

- giving opinions

- imposing your beliefs or emotions

- judging

- making suggestions.

Why counsel people?
Most people are capable of sorting out their own problems and crises. Some aren't. For these people, just talking things over with someone can be a great help.

How to counsel someone
If someone has a problem and wants to talk it over with you, always remember the following:

- Accept and tolerate their confusion.

- Allow the person to make their own decision.

- Check you understand, and confirm you are both on the same wavelength.

- Empathise with them – try to see things through their eyes.

- Establish the facts and what options they have.

- Give the person encouragement and confidence to keep talking.

- Give the person the space they need to explore the

problem for themselves. This means not talking too much.

- Leave a way open for the person to talk to you again if they wish.

- Make the person feel you are there for them.

- Open up other avenues of thought they may not have considered.

- Respond in a genuine, caring manner.

- Say you are pleased they felt able to talk to you.

- Show interest.

- Show you understand their difficulty.

- Stress confidentiality.

- Try and clarify confused thoughts.

What to avoid

Try not to do any of the following:

- Appear shocked by anything that is said.

- Come up with premature suggestions.

- Discuss the person with others (unless they agree you may).

- Give advice or express your own views.

- Let your own values, perceptions and attitudes get in the way.

- Make the person feel inferior or inadequate.

- Make personal judgements.

- Stop the free flow of conversation.

MANAGEMENT TIPS

- Appraise people regularly – informally as well as formally.

- Always take employee complaints and/or grievances seriously.

- Deal with performance problems as soon as they arise.

- Always be seen to be fair.

- Remember, discipline is not about judgement or punishment. It is about getting performance right – closing the gap.

- Make time for people – counselling doesn't have to be formal. Listen to people and show an interest – sometimes it can help a great deal.

ACTION POINTS

1. Choose a member of staff at work, and imagine you have to appraise them next week. Objectively assess their performance in terms of past, present and future.

2. Choose a member of staff with a real or imaginary performance problem. Identify the gap, and think of how you could establish this gap so they accept it exists. How would you establish the reasons for the gap – what would you ask them? Set some objectives to close the gap.

3. Imagine that the performance problem has not improved. How does your organisation's disciplinary process tell you to proceed?

10

Managing Customers

UNDERSTANDING CUSTOMERS AND SERVICE

Your customers are your organisation's reason for existing. Whether you have individual customers purchasing goods and services from you, or have other organisations who obtain goods and services from you, or just deal with staff from other parts of your organisation (called **internal customers**) – customer service is important.

Whenever you deal with people outside your work, whether face-to-face, by telephone or in writing, you should remember one thing – the **image** of your work. You *are* your organisation as far as the other person is concerned. How you react to them will influence their view of your organisation as a whole – it will affect your organisation's image.

Customer service is often referred to as **customer care**.

What makes good customer care?

- Courteous staff.

- Friendly staff.

- Helpful (but not pushy) staff.

- Informative staff, who keep customers informed without needing to be chased.

- Knowledgeable staff.

- Professional staff.

- Responsible staff.

- Staff who behave as if they care about the customer.

- Staff who do not lose their ability to perform under pressure.

- Staff who do not reduce the service they offer under pressure.

- Staff who do what they say they will.

- Staff who listen.

- Staff who promote a good image of their product, service, work or organisation.

- Staff who respond promptly.

Spot the obvious? The word **staff** appears every time. Yes, people come to you for a product or service, but what makes them remember your organisation is the staff. The best product or service can be ruined by the worst staff, and vice versa.

The importance of internal customers

We are often so keen to deal well with those outside the organisation that we neglect our internal customers. Late information, non-returned telephone calls, unanswered internal memos all indicate poor customer care to internal customers. And the most ironic thing is that they may need your information or answer in order to service a 'real', external customer of their own – you end up providing bad service to those you wanted to serve best.

CASE STUDY

Nikki neglects her internal customers

Nikki receives a memo from marketing, and then the phone rings. A credit company is asking for financial information, and this is swiftly followed by a complaint from a customer. She deals with the complaint and credit company first. By the time she gets round to the marketing memo, she has already been given several messages chasing a response. By the time she responds, it is the following day, and marketing lose a big order because the customer decides to give their business to someone else.

Nikki needs to remember that internal customers are as important as external ones. She should have checked how urgent their query was – not just prioritised it as unimportant simply because it was internal.

DEALING WITH PEOPLE BY TELEPHONE

- Answer the telephone as quickly as possible.

- Give telephone calls your full attention – don't read or carry on with other work whilst speaking.

- Identify yourself by name, section, job title or the form your organisation usually uses.

- If the right person isn't available, offer to take a message – don't wait to be asked.

- If you have to put someone on hold:
  – explain why
  – reassure them now and again that you haven't forgotten them
  – thank them for waiting once you take their call back
  – never put someone on hold without asking their permission first.

- Keep information handy – have information to hand before making a call.

- Listen not only to what they say, but *how* they say it – remember you can't see them, so you need to listen for clues as to how they are feeling.

- On the telephone, you cannot see the other person, and they cannot see you. Always remember this, and try to sound friendly, approachable, professional and all the other things you would like them to see if they could see you. Try visualising them sat facing you, and speak as you would to their face.

- Transfer calls as little as possible – always try to deal with things if you can, because most people hate being transferred. If you have to transfer a call, tell the customer who you are putting them through to. In addition, if you can, tell the recipient of the call a little about the customer, to avoid them having to repeat themselves.

CASE STUDY

Bev deals with an angry relative

One morning, Sheila answers the phone. The sister of a resident is asking how she is. Sheila puts her on hold while she goes and finds Bev. By the time Bev gets to the phone, the caller is furious. 'I'm in a phone box!' she says, 'I'd have called back if I'd known how long it was going to be! As it was, I kept putting more money in, expecting someone to speak to me at any second!'

All Bev can do at this stage is apologise. Sheila should have asked whether the caller was happy to hold. Bev needs to train everyone in phone procedures – which are common sense to some people, but new to others.

COMMUNICATING WITH PEOPLE IN WRITING

Letters have three main functions:

- to give information
- to get information
- to get something done.

They also need to create in the mind of the reader the impression that the writer and their organisation are efficient, helpful, professional and polite. Always ensure your letters are not only accurate but also written with the right tone.

Who are you writing to?

You don't always know who you are writing to. That is, you don't always know their age, language or intelligence. They may know about your organisation, or they may not. You need to take this into account, and write clearly and simply, without using technical terms, jargon or abbreviations.

When to write

- Always write promptly.

- Write when it is more appropriate than telephoning or seeing the person.

- Write when you have information they need.

- Write when you want to ask questions.

What do people want to know in a letter?

- Who it is from (your name, nor just your job title).

- Where it is from.

- Where to reply to.

- When to reply by.

- Who to telephone in case of query.

Signs of a good letter

- A heading saying what the letter is about.

- An introduction.

- Broken into short paragraphs.

- Clear, simple writing.

- Concluded with a summary of what the recipient needs to do.

- Gives the impression the writer knows what they are talking about.

- Gives a good image of the organisation.

- Short and to the point – not padded out with irrelevant information.

- Smart – no mistakes or corrections.

- Polite.

- Truthful.

- Written in a logical order.

QUESTIONS AND ANSWERS

My work only ever deals with internal customers. Is customer care really that important for me?
Yes. Every manager has customers, whether internal or external. For some departments, such as sales or marketing, dealing with external customers is a major part of their job. Other managers, in what we call **service departments** (such as personnel, finance and computing) only deal with internal customers. But service departments are there to service the other departments. And without that service, sales and marketing, and other departments that regularly deal with external customers, cannot do their job. They can't provide good service to *their* customers.

So how can I improve customer care?
By setting a good example, and setting high standards for your staff. Be **proactive**. This means taking the initiative, and not waiting to be asked to do things. You could set standards for responses. Ideas for this would be:

- answering telephones within four rings

- answering all letters or memos within five days

- answering telephone messages within two days etc.

156

HANDLING COMPLAINTS

Complaints worry most people. However, they give us feedback from customers, so we can make improvements. Thus, we can use them to improve our customer care.

Two things are needed for handling complaints:

- a good attitude

- good procedures.

Developing a good attitude

- Be responsible.

- Do not respond aggressively.

- Don't be defensive.

- Establish the facts, by asking questions where necessary.

- Give the complainant time to express how they feel.

- If necessary, help them express themselves.

- Keep any promises you make, and don't make any you can't keep.

- Listen actively.

- Never assign blame – people don't want to know whose fault it is, they just want to know what you are going to do about it.

- Never just say 'no' – always explain.

- Respond as soon as possible.

- Show interest.

- Stay calm.

- Stay objective.

- Tell the customer what you are going to do about the complaint.

Developing good procedures

- Even if the customer is right, don't undermine your staff.

- If you have to overrule a member of staff, explain why, so they don't feel undermined.

- Give people authority to handle complaints where they need it.

- Have clear procedures.

- Make sure the procedures are known by all staff.

- Record all complaints so you can see any patterns.

CASE STUDY

Mike undermines his staff

Sam has a complaint about some information she has supplied to a manager in another department. She is unable to resolve it by phone, so the manager says he will take it up with Mike, her boss. She tells Mike what happened, and he promises to deal with it. When the manager arrives to see Mike, Sam again tries to help, but he will only deal with Mike. Mike agrees things will be put right, and apologises for the 'mistake'. When the other manager has gone, he says, 'Sorry Sam, I know you were in the right, but I needed to smooth things over, all right?' 'No it isn't!' snaps Sam, 'You made me look small and stupid! What's the point in my dealing with things if you just come and back down and give in to people, as if I was wrong in the first place?'

Mike should remember not to undermine his staff when dealing with complaints. Just because the customer is always right, he need not accept that his staff was in the wrong! When his staff are right, he needs to explain that they *are* right, but that he is going to sort things out to please the other person. That way, he doesn't undermine the status of other people.

APPRECIATING CONSUMER LEGISLATION

If you sell or receive goods on behalf of your organisation, you need to know what your legal rights and obligations are.

Understanding contracts

When someone buys something from someone else, they are entering into a **contract**. This contract has two parts. The first part is the customer's offer to buy at a certain price. The second part is the supplier's acceptance of the order and/or agreement to sell.

When both parts are completed, we say there is a **binding contract**. This simply means that neither party can change their minds or alter the contract terms.

Knowing about the legislation

Three Acts form the relevant legislation in England and Wales (the legislation in Scotland and Northern Ireland is slightly different). These Acts are:

- Sale of Goods Act 1979

- Trade Descriptions Act 1968

- Consumer Protection Act 1987.

The Sale of Goods Act 1979

Goods must be:

- as described

- of merchantable quality

- fit for the purpose for which they are intended.

If goods fail to comply
If goods do not comply with all three criteria, the purchaser is entitled to a refund.

- The seller does not have to offer anything but a cash

refund, but the buyer can accept a replacement or repair if offered.

- The buyer does not have to accept a credit note.

- 'No refund' notices are illegal.

- Second-hand goods are covered by the Act, but refunds depend on a number of things like age of item, price paid etc.

- Sale items are included, but if the price was reduced because of damage, the buyer cannot later complain about that damage.

- The buyer does not legally have to produce a receipt, but the buyer can be asked for proof of purchase, e.g. cheque stub, credit card slip etc.

- The buyer is not entitled to a refund if they change their mind, decide that something does not fit, or damage the item themselves.

- The buyer is not entitled to a refund if they were aware of the fault or should have seen it, or if they did not purchase the item themselves.

The Trade Descriptions Act 1968
This relates to false descriptions of goods. A seller who gives a false description of goods is breaking the law.

The Consumer Protection Act 1987
This Act covers two offences. Firstly, sellers cannot give misleading information about prices. Secondly, goods cannot be supplied which are not reasonably safe.

MANAGEMENT TIPS
- Be attentive to people:
  - listen
  - ask questions
  - take notes

- concentrate
- don't interrupt.

- Be proactive:
  - volunteer information
  - offer a choice wherever possible
  - point out things people may not have noticed.

- Be accurate:
  - never guess
  - find out information you don't know
  - use people's names wherever possible
  - know the law – and keep within it.

ACTION POINTS

1. Think of a time when you have had poor delivery of goods or services as an internal customer from people within your organisation. What went wrong and why? Do you cause similar problems to your internal customers? What can you do about it?

2. Think of a time when you have complained. How well was your complaint handled? Are you satisfied with the way the complaint was handled? What can you learn from this about how your organisation handles complaints?

11

Managing Change

UNDERSTANDING CHANGE

Most of us live in a world of constant change. Changes in technology, employment, finance, legislation and many other things have altered the world we live and work in. Any organisation is changing all the time – the structures, systems, procedures, lines of authority and people working there are all changing.

Appreciating different types of change

Change occurs on many different scales, from small everyday changes to major changes in your organisation and how it works.

Everyday (routine) changes
These are the sort of changes that managers face every day. They are routine problem-solving exercises. This doesn't mean they don't require big decisions, or cost a lot of money, but it does mean that they are not going to change the organisation radically. Examples would be a person resigning, a machine breaking down, or a customer complaint resulting in new procedures to prevent it happening again.

Emergency changes (crises)
These are sudden crises that occur without warning and require a change to cope with them. A good example would be a strike or industrial dispute, a corporate take-over, or a supplier going out of business.

Improvement changes (innovation)
These occur all the time in good organisations, as

managers see better, easier ways to do things. Examples would be new product development, introduction of computerised systems, or introduction of new procedures.

Radical changes (transformations)
This is where organisations change their entire way of doing things. This may be deliberate, or a forced response to a huge crisis. Examples would be privatisation of a public utility, a merger with another company, or closure of a large part of an organisation.

Sequence of change
Fig. 16 shows the sequence of change.

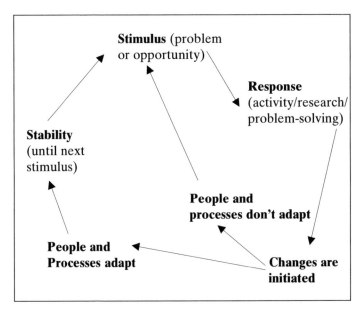

Fig. 16. The sequence of change.

HANDLING CHANGE

When a change occurs, or you have decided a change may be necessary, and you are going to handle things yourself, a good sequence for handling change is the sequence we used for decision-making:

1. Define the problem or issue that may indicate the need for change.
2. Gather information.
3. Create options.
4. Evaluate options.
5. Decide on the best course of action: what change to make and how.
6. Implement your decision – implement the change(s).
7. Follow up and evaluate.

CASE STUDY

Mike's team suggests unnecessary changes

Mike is having a new computer system installed (again). He calls in the team and talks with them about it. They have a range of ideas, and people get very enthusiastic about the change. Mike takes the ideas to his own manager, who is less enthusiastic, 'These ideas are a little radical,' he says, 'Let's just stick with getting the system in, shall we?'

Mike understands this is an innovative change, but once people got enthusiastic, it started to become rather more radical and adventurous. People are wary of too much change at once, and Mike needs to remember this.

QUESTIONS AND ANSWERS

So is change a good thing?
Sometimes, sometimes not. The old saying 'if it ain't broke, don't fix it' is a good one. On the other hand, just because it isn't broken, doesn't mean that things wouldn't work better after a few changes. If a change is imposed on you and it is for the worse, try to accept it – little is gained by fighting it, and your staff will probably follow your lead.

Surely people can see good change will benefit them, so there won't be any problems?
Not necessarily. Even when a change is to someone's advantage, they rarely accept it without comment. Sometimes people oppose something 'out of principle'.

Is managing change always the manager's job then?
Yes – managing is a manager's job. However, to manage change, you need to involve people and communicate, so it isn't necessary that you cope alone. Talk to people – let them know what is going on, and don't be afraid to ask for help and/or suggestions.

RESISTING CHANGE

People often resist change. How hard they resist it can be plotted on a scale, as shown in Fig. 17.

MANAGING RESISTANCE TO CHANGE

Reasons for resisting change
There are many reasons why people may resist change. If you are faced with resistance, try to discover which of them apply:

- Fear
    - of experimenting
    - of failure
    - of looking stupid
    - of loss of power
    - of loss of skills and/or expertise
    - of problems
    - of redundancy
    - of the unknown.

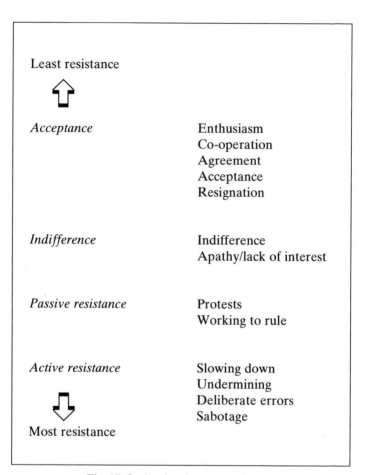

Fig. 17. Scale of resistance to change.

- Lack
  - of good working relationships
  - of information
  - of involvement
  - of security
  - of trust
  - of understanding of the need for change.

- Information issues
  - erroneous information
  - ignorance
  - rumours.

- Reasoning
  - clinging to the status quo – inflexibility
  - erroneous thinking
  - habit
  - historical experience
  - inability to see the benefits
  - love of conformity.

CASE STUDY

Nikki introduces a new way of handling accounts

Nikki and her team are told that the company has taken over a smaller company, and soon their accounts will be coming to Nikki's office in addition to their usual ones. Everyone can see it will be very difficult to cope with the extra figures and paperwork. Nikki tries to see how the workload can be accommodated. She decides to make each team member responsible for a stage in the process, which they will become practised in, and thus quicker. Excitedly, she realises that all their accounts can be handled this way, and explains the new system to the team. She is surprised when they all respond differently. Bill is enthusiastic, and sees an opportunity to specialise. Peter doesn't care – he just wants to get on with what he's told. Jacquie isn't happy, and makes a fuss but eventually gives in, whilst Lyn and David seem to be being deliberately awkward.

Nikki needs to remember that people react differently to change. She needs to allow for this, and consult and communicate with people whilst her ideas are taking shape, not just when she has made a final decision. That way, they will feel involved.

Overcoming resistance to change

You can overcome resistance to change only with effort.
You need to make time for people, to try to ensure they
see the change(s) in the right way.

Preparation
- Be positive.

- Check for training needs – will people need training?

- Ensure adequate resources are available to make the
  change go smoothly.

- Get the timing right wherever possible.

- Set clear objectives.

Information
- Be sure of your facts.

- Check things out – 'look before you leap'.

- Check what things don't need to change, and make sure
  they aren't being affected.

- Look at things from all angles.

Involvement
- Ask for views and feedback.

- Delegate where possible – it involves people.

- Get those affected to participate in making decisions if
  possible.

- Get to know people.

- Involve experts. This does not have to be consultants –
  some of your own staff may have specialist or in-depth
  knowledge.

Communication
- Be honest.

- Don't withhold information – tell people as much as you can.

- Encourage two-way communication.

- Explain the circumstances that create the need for change.

- Make the change sound achievable and sensible.

- Sell people the change – don't force it on them.

Awareness
- Encourage people.

- Keep aware of the changes and how they are going.

- Recognise effort and contribution.

- Recognise that resistance is healthy and natural, and work to overcome it.

- Review and check the change works.

- Squash rumours wherever possible.

CASE STUDY

Bev's staff are unhappy about change
Bev is told in future everyone must work in pairs. She has no idea why, and everyone is very angry – they feel they are no longer trusted.

Bev needs to work to overcome their resistance to the change. By finding out the reasons, she might be able to explain things to them. Even if not, she needs to sell the benefits of the new arrangement, so people are motivated to cooperate.

MANAGEMENT TIPS

- Take time to do things properly – change takes time, and so does managing it.

- Use your strengths – use the best people where they will be best able to help you.

- Allocate enough resources – don't underestimate how long a change will take.

- Communicate.

- Involve people as early on and as extensively as possible.

ACTION POINTS

1. Think of the worst change you could be asked to make at work. Why does it worry you so much? What could your manager do to relieve your anxiety?

2. Identify a major change that has happened at work. How was it handled? How could it have been handled better?

12

Managing Your Career

UNDERSTANDING MANAGEMENT QUALIFICATIONS

There are many academic management qualifications which can be gained at colleges, universities and other training providers. The most common are:

- Certificate in Supervisory Management (CSM)

- Certificate in Management (CIM or CM)

- Certificate in Management Studies (CMS)

- Diploma in Management (DM)

- Diploma in Management Studies (DMS)

- Master in Business Administration (MBA)

Entry requirements usually depend on a mixture of qualifications, management position and experience. Most of these qualifications are assessed by a mixture of coursework and examinations, to test your skills and knowledge.

OPTIONS FOR STUDY

There are three main options:

- full-time

- part-time

- distance learning (correspondence course).

Full-time study

Advantages
- The place at which you study will probably have library, computing and other facilities for you to use.

- You may benefit from a secondment or placement with an employer.

- You will benefit from regular contact with fellow students.

- You will be able to have regular contact with your teachers.

- You can devote all your time to the course.

Disadvantages
- You will have to pay study fees and will be unable to work full-time.

- Few employers will sponsor employees on long full-time courses.

- Unless you have a work placement, you have little or no opportunity to try out your academic learning in a real workplace.

Part-time study
This is similar to full-time study, but the teaching normally occurs for one day or one afternoon and evening per week.

Advantages
- There is access to facilities.

- You can continue your job and thus protect your income.

- Many employers are happy with this sort of study, often referred to as **day release**.

Disadvantages
- There is less opportunity for group work and discussions, as time is limited.

- You need to attend regularly, so your employer will need to agree to this, unless you can attend out of working hours.

- As class time is limited, you usually need to commit yourself to a great deal of self-study, which needs discipline.

Distance learning
The most common form of this is a correspondence course. You buy the materials needed for study as part of your course, and work to a set programme. Most such courses provide a tutor with whom you can correspond (hence the name correspondence course). They will mark your work, or **assignments**.

Advantages
- You are not tied to certain times of attendance.

- No time off work is required, unless there are exams or a residential part of the course.

Disadvantages
- It can be hard to motivate yourself to study alone.

- You lack contact with other students.

- Practical subjects such as interviewing or counselling can be difficult to cover – you can get the information, but have no opportunity to practise.

DECIDING ON OPTIONS

The following questions, if you think carefully about them, should help you decide which course of study is best for you.

- Does the course provide any materials?

- How many books and other things will you need to buy or have access to?

- How many people will be on the course and who are they?

- How much face-to-face contact with instuctors is there?

- How much study time is required, apart from class time?

- Is there any flexibility if you have to slow down your study for any reason for a period of time?

- Is there support if you are struggling with part of the course?

- What level of attendance is required?

- Who are the course teachers?

MANAGEMENT TIPS

- Think carefully about what is the best qualification for you.

- Think about how best to study – full-time, part-time or by distance learning.

- Look carefully at places that do the course you want.

Index